Relationship Matters is a timely invitation and inspiring guide for what it means to live an empowered and purposeful life in relationship with others. For all of us, the role of our family connections and relationships are and have been an important influence in developing what we value and who are today. In an insightful and practical way, Mark has outlined 5 critical pillars that provide a roadmap and strategic action plan for individuals wanting to create a family environment that is transformational in the way it supports its members to become healthy, content, competent and flourishing adults. Drawing upon his own life experiences, Mark illustrates the key building blocks to developing genuine connectedness with others based upon the guiding values and strengths-based principles required to experience a healthy relational home environment. What makes Mark's invitation unique is the paradigm shift away from managing one's relationships out of fear to purposefully growing the innate potential of flourishing in relationship with others as the key to what makes life meaningful and fulfilling. This is a book that invites one to consider the critical role of genuine relationships and how a family environment can nurture the essential resilience, strengths and sense of optimism required for its members to thrive in an unpredictable and challenging world.

Wayne Hammond, Ph.D.
Founding Partner and CSO
Flourishing Life
Adjunct Professor at Ambrose University

RELATIONSHIP
MATTERS

The Essential Blueprint to
**Building Strong Families &
Fostering Healthy Relationships**

MARK GORDON

FriesenPress

Suite 300 - 990 Fort St
Victoria, BC, V8V 3K2
Canada

www.friesenpress.com

I would like to acknowledge the foundational principals and some illustrations were learned while working with Jack Toth at Impact Society.

Michelle King (initial read over and made suggestions)

ISBN
978-1-5255-7435-1 (Hardcover)
978-1-5255-7436-8 (Paperback)
978-1-5255-7437-5 (eBook)

1. Family & Relationships, Marriage

Distributed to the trade by The Ingram Book Company

TABLE OF CONTENTS

ACKNOWLEDGMENTS

As you will read there are three things that are very important to me, faith, family and friendships. I would have no content to write without all three of those in my life, so I would like to thank the following people who have made my life what it is, and helping me write this book.

FAITH

Jesus for His love and direction in my life and for the passion he has put in my heart for serving others, without him I can do nothing, with him I have done more than I could have ever imagined.

FAMILY

My wife Sandi, of 37 years (at the time of publishing), is who gives me courage and permission to dream and to take her on crazy adventures. Thank you for sticking with me through all the hard times and celebrating during the good. You are the glue for our family and have inspired me in so many ways. I love you and love our life together.

My children and grandchildren who bring me so much joy. You have taught me what grace is and what it means to follow a dream. I am proud of each of you, you are people of character and integrity and have lived out the principals I share in this book. Your support of each other is inspiring enough, but your support of mom and I has been stellar. I am humbled to be your dad/grandpa and so overjoyed with the honour. Justen & Kristin,

Jelene, Zach, Violet and Jude, Jenna & Nick you are amazing, and I love you deeply!!

I am so grateful for my extended family, my sister Ruth and all my nephews and nieces and great nephews and nieces, my wife's family especially her mom Carol – I love you all and always will. To my dad, mom, and brothers John and Billy – I miss you deeply but know your enjoying heaven together.

FRIENDSHIPS

My best friend Chris and his wife Lori, I am so grateful for the relationship we have, the countless hours of tears, laughter and silliness has been so rich in my life. The support you have shown and the feedback you have provided in my life is irreplaceable. In life there may only be a very few friends that are closer than brothers and stand with you no matter what you may be going through and Chris you are one of them for me!

Jack and Collette, you have been a model family to look to for inspiration for many but especially for me. Jack all the years we dreamed together and shared revelation with each other has found its way onto to the pages of this book. The years we worked together in developing the Heroes program were some of the best years of my life. Thank you for writing the forward and your ongoing friendship.

Big Jim you are a friend, a big brother and a role model all wrapped up into one big teddy bear. Thanks for being a mentor and thanks for the size 16's to the butt you gave me when I needed it most. I would not be where I am without you.

My church family at the Bridge I love you and appreciate each of you. To all the leaders who have walked with me through the years and to the people who have served faithfully… You are amazing and have been a huge blessing to me and my family. Thank you, Michelle King, for your editing in the early stages, your work was stellar, and it really helped me write this book. Emily King thank you for sharing your art for this book.

FORWARD

From the moment I picked up Mark Gordon's manuscript, I was impacted with the truths written. Upon completion, I am more convinced than ever that every parent, couple, leader, teacher, and young person should read it. I believe Mark has achieved the rare ability to create a "how to" book with an emotional connection.

Mark is a gifted, relational communicator. Throughout this book, you will hear the desire of his heart to be a people builder. You will be struck by his honesty and encouraged through his personal lessons and observations. Walking with Mark through this book will lead you to understand how you can turn challenges into building blocks that will equip you and help those you influence. These learnings, combined with Mark's easily implemented relationship tools, will have you living life on a deeper level.

Above all, you will be inspired to see the fulfillment that can happen through family. Mark's love and passion for family will have you perceiving differently, like putting on a pair of prescription glasses for the first time. You will see more clearly what, has always been around you, as well as the pathways to pursue and the pitfalls to avoid. This will enable you, your family, and those you influence to enjoy all you are designed and created for.

Jack Toth
Founder/CEO IMPACT Society
Author Canadian Best-Selling Book "The Teacher Every Student Wants and Needs".

Authors note – There will be a donation towards Impact Society programs from every book sold. Thank you for investing in young people and their families by buying this book. As I believe every family should have this book in their hands, I am offering bulk pricing for organizations to purchase for families they serve. For more information about bulk purchasing and pricing, email mark@markgordon.ca

RELATIONSHIP
MATTERS

MARK GORDON

PREFACE

This book comes from my passion to see families learn how to facilitate healthy and loving homes for children to grow up in, homes that have a relationally healthy culture that are rich in love and purpose. My heart breaks when I see how people are affected when they don't grow up in this type of home. It is amazing when a child grows up in a home that affirms their personhood and encourages them to live with purpose! Parents who are not providing this kind of home were, at one time, kids who did not grow up in one. My life's mission and the writing of this book are to help break that cycle by providing principles and tools to families, so they can enjoy a vibrant, healthy home.

It was the middle of the night. I was tired and cold as I sat staring at the concrete wall across from me. It stared back, reflecting my cold and empty heart. An iron door slammed shut, startling me back to reality. I was fifteen, sitting in a jail cell, feeling scared and alone. Questions raced through my mind as if on a mission to find all of life's answers. How did I get here? How could I have lost my way so profoundly? I came from a good home. I had every opportunity to do well in life, but there I sat as a high-school dropout and a drug addict, alone and cold.

I wish I could tell you that this moment was a wake-up call and that, like a phoenix, I pulled my life together and rose triumphantly from the ashes. However, although that eventually happened, there were many more years of self-inflicted pain and hurting others before I found my way. In time, I was able to realize that not only was I sitting in ashes, but I was the one who had started the fire. What I came to understand through all of my experiences was that I was terrible at relating to people. I did not know how to build and maintain a relationship with anyone.

Many things played a part in my inglorious fall, but pain from broken relationships is what primarily led me to that cell. Building relationships was just not a skill that was taught, at least not in my parent's house. I have come to realize that most people have not been taught the skills needed to build a healthy relational culture at home or work. This is tragic because relationships affect every area of our lives. Relationships are hard work, but they are also vital to a happy and content life. Relationships help guide us to make healthy choices and to pick us up when we don't. Although I grew up in a good home, it was one where rules were more important than connection. Because I could not live up to the standard rules created, I grew up thinking I was a failure.

What's the one thing every person in the world has in common? Relationships! That's right. Unless you live on a mountain, off the grid, you cannot avoid having relationships. Even then, you would have to relate to yourself and the mountain you are hiding on. So, rather than fumble through life hoping your relationships work out, it is important to learn how to create healthy relationships. Learning this skill will enrich your life and create that sense of connectedness that is seriously lacking in our society. Everyone is looking for acceptance and significance, and the main source of both is relationships. People can be the most rewarding thing in your life but also the most difficult and painful. We were created with an inherent need to relate with others. It is a built-in desire, which, unfulfilled, can cause us to experience extreme pain and loneliness. This was the case for me for many years because I thought a good relationship looked like me getting what I wanted. But relationships require investment and effort. When I began to value the relationships in my life and give them the right priority, I started to actually enjoy them.

Close your eyes for a moment and imagine a theatre. Visualize the stage, an audience, and the props that help tell the story. Look around; what is closest to you? Look out at the audience; what do you see? Try a see the people in your life standing or sitting in the theater with you. Using this visualization, you can associate the playhouse with the following four levels of relationship:

- On stage – inner circle
- Front row – cheerleaders
- General audience – acquaintances
- Back row – the public

As you might expect, the level of connection in the relationship determines the investment required to make it a good one. The people who influence you the most are the ones you allow to be in your inner circle, on stage or cheerleaders in the front row. What they say and how they treat you makes a huge difference in your life. At times, there are people in your life you have allowed to sit on stage with you or in the front row, but they have not supported or invested in you. You allow them to influence you in the wrong ways. If they are negative voices in your life, rather than fighting to force them to love you, you may want to move them further back into your audience. The people you want to invest your relational equity in are those who have consistently displayed the ability to cheer you on and be there with you in life including times of trouble. It is ok to have people in the audience even in the back row that you don't have consistent contact with, just make sure that the people closest, who have the most influence are investing in you as much as you in them.

My wife and I could not have come from more different backgrounds or family dynamics. If you were to look at our families from the outside and make a judgment, you would probably conclude that her family was dysfunctional and mine was normal. However, if you peeled back the surface, you would discover that both have had a lot of dysfunction, just in very different ways.

In my family, my parents had an external pressure to present a perfect family, and this pressure caused a lot of pain within my family. My dad was a minister in an era that said if your family was not perfect, you were not worthy to be a minister. As a result, there was a tremendous amount of pressure put on my dad to have a perfect family. When I was a child, I had people tell me that I was a disgrace to my dad's ministry simply because I was hyperactive. This certainly was not God's thought or idea, but it hurt my family and me. Unfortunately, it also shaped the concept of my identity as well, one that was rooted in fear and self-hatred.

My parents made decisions that they came to regret years later concerning discipline and what we kids were allowed to do and not do. This, of course, caused pain and division within the family. Each of my siblings and I acted out in different ways that had negative outcomes.

In my wife's case, there was alcohol abuse in her household. She and her siblings were each affected differently, but in the end, all were hurt by the results of alcohol abuse. It caused violence and rejection to enter into the home and caused tremendous pain for all concerned. Thankfully both families have grown and healed, we now enjoy wonderful times together and understand how to express our love for each other much better.

The fact is every family has dysfunction in it. If you peeled back the surface of any family, you would see some form of dysfunction or pain because there is no perfect family. The ones that look the best to society can often be most dysfunctional, or at least they hide it the best. Now, please, don't hear what I'm not saying. There are many healthy and loving families out there, including the family my wife and I have created with our children. However, everyone has some struggle to go through within their family, and all of them have a few things they need to do to ensure that they develop a healthy relational culture in their homes. The truth is that relationships can't grow in depth without some friction and struggle. I am grateful that both of our families have reconciled and can express love to each other today. We have seen many miracles and healings. There is always hope when you keep your heart open to forgiveness and healing. A family can build resilience in its relationships through the principles I will share in this book.

My hope is that this book will help you do the following three things:

1. Discover the importance of intentional investment in relationships.
2. Give you an investment strategy.
3. Provide a step-by-step plan on how to execute this strategy.

If we compare a resilient home with the house that contains it, that house needs three distinct things to make the have good bones. Similarly, if we want relationships and families to have good bones, they need a *healthy foundation*, to build on, a *strong framework* that allows the relationships to prosper, and a *sturdy roof* or covering to keep it safe in the storms of life we all face.

In this book, we will unpack how to build all three of these distinctive elements to create a healthy relational culture at home. It is an essential guide to building a strong family and fostering healthy relationships.

SECTION 1
BUILDING A HEALTHY FOUNDATION

In the first section we look at building a healthy foundation, when building a house, the foundation holds the full weight of that house. The bigger the house the stronger the foundation needs to be. To build a home with healthy relationships it is the same, for a healthy relational culture to flourish you need a healthy foundation within your relationships. There are five pillars that build strength into your relationships and in this section, we will look at all five in detail.

THE FIVE PILLARS

There is a skyscraper in San Francisco that leans to one side a little more every year. It has become so pronounced you can actually see it list with the naked eye. They have called engineers from around the world to try and solve its tilt. They discovered that the pillars that were originally driven down into the dirt were not put in properly, and the weight of the building has caused the foundation to sink on one side. Not unlike this building's foundation, which suffers because of a particular weakness, your relationships need pillars that are driven deep into the heart and culture of your family's relationships to provide the strength needed to safely support the weight of every relationship in the whole family.

When creating healthy relationships, we start by looking at how to build a healthy foundation. The bigger the house, the stronger the foundation has to be. In the same way, a relationship is only as strong as the quality of its foundation. There are five pillars to a healthy foundation that support the whole structure of a family culture. The level of relationship will determine the amount of time you invest, but the five pillars, which make up a solid foundation, will create healthy relationships no matter which level you're on.

These five pillars are the footings of a healthy foundation:

1. Trust – can hold the weight of a relationship, but takes time to build
2. Communication – expresses the value of the relationship
3. Authenticity – allows everyone to see their own contribution to relationship
4. Honesty – keeps the relationship open and helps build trust
5. Honour – lifts up each person in the relationship

These five pillars interact with each other, and all five have to be acted on to create a healthy environment in which a relationship can flourish. In my experience of working with people who have failed relationships, most have no understanding concerning the foundational principles of relationships and have unconsciously sabotaged their relationship right from the beginning. This has broken one or more of the pillars, which has in turned undermined the strength of relationships.

CHAPTER 1
PILLAR 1 – TRUST

"Mark, clean your room up before you go out to play!" my mom yelled out. Of course," I replied, "Sure, Mom." But then, I threw a couple of shirts from the floor to the bed and promptly ran out to play with my friends. After a few days, I was told I would not be going out to play that day. I was so angry. I threw a temper tantrum, feeling like the world was unfair and that my mom must hate me. What I failed to see was that it had nothing to do with me not cleaning my room. The issue was that I had broken trust by saying one thing and doing another. From then on, I always had to have my mom check my room before I went out with my friends. I felt untrusted and undeservedly punished. But I could have stopped the whole thing by doing what I said I would.

Every relationship at any level starts with trust. It is an essential ingredient in a healthy relationship. It is the first pillar in the foundation because it can hold the weight of a relationship even when things go wrong. Trust is something that does not happen by accident. It needs to be intentionally worked on, talked about, and invested in. It is like a savings account that you make deposits into. Money is saved up, so when you need to make a withdrawal, the money is there to spend. If you make only withdrawals and never deposits, you will eventually go into overdraft and ultimately go bankrupt. So it is with relationships; they require trust equity to thrive. Relationships are not unlike equity in your financial life. Financial equity is the value of your assets minus the cost of acquiring them. It takes years of making wise, intentional, financial decisions to build up enough equity to have the resources to achieve your financial goals in life. In the same way, trust equity is always developed over time. We need to invest intentionally in our relationships in order to see a return on the investment. I have found it handy to have some extra equity, so when I mess up – and believe me I do that regularly – I don't 'break the bank!' In other words, if I have built trust and then make a mistake within a relationship, I have a greater opportunity to ask for and receive forgiveness.

Society in general has a trust crisis, we can see it in the business world through the sacrifice of ethics. We can see it in the political world by politicians making promises and not following through. We also see it in the media with fake news phenomena and all of this rubs off on our personal relationships. When trust is broken in one area of life, the brokenness tends to bleed into other areas and has a negative effect on our home life. It seems with the busyness of our lives today that it is difficult to build the trust required to cultivate healthy relationships. I have seen so many families break apart because trust is broken over and over. On the surface, it seems easier to walk away and start over again. However, I have found that it's actually easier to make the necessary investment to create health in the relationship than to have a path full of failed ones and always having to start over. Each time we walk away rather than invest, it becomes more difficult to build trust in the next relationship. You simply carry the broken trust forward to the next relationship. Recently, a friend made decisions without considering how it might affect other people, including me. To be honest, I was just plain mad. I was hurt and really just wanted to walk away and say, "Oh well, whatever!" Then I began to think about all the time I had invested into this relationship and how much I valued it. I decided to choose relationship over offence. Because I had built a lot of trust equity with him, I felt safe to talk about the whole situation. To my amazement, he listened and even thanked me. If I had chosen the easier path of walking away, I could have carried the offence into my other relationships. Which in turn, could make it hard for me to trust others.

WHAT BUILDS TRUST EQUITY?

There are a few things that make deposits into the trust bank within a relationship. Intentional investment through *transparency*, *loyalty*, and *fulfilled promises* provide the necessary deposits.".

Transparency

Trust is built when you can see into someone's heart, which is transparency. This will be where we see the trust pillar grow. Every hidden thing, regardless of size, erodes trust. It is important to bring things into the open as much and as soon as possible. Transparency goes beyond just being honest. It is being real or being honest with who you are on the inside. It is keeping your heart open to one another. Often, when developing a relationship, we are tempted to pretend that we are something we are not in order to gain approval. When the relationship becomes serious, we have to keep up the façade because we become fearful that the person will walk away when they see the real you. Transparency protects you from having to remember what you said or pretended to be. If people don't love you for you, who do they love? Because transparency means that you have been real and open, it helps build trust equity. Then, when you make a mistake and need to make a withdrawal from the trust bank to overcome the mistake, you have the resources you need. You have the trust equity to help rebuild when an area of relationship is wounded. Being real and open builds trust equity, it is that simple but not always easy.

Loyalty

Loyalty is not talked about much in today's culture; we seem to have forgotten its value. Loyalty in its purest form is to be faithful and devoted to someone. I was having a conversation with a client, who is also a friend, the other day regarding his brand. He was lamenting that the only loyalty nowadays is to price. There was a time when people were dedicated because of the quality and consistency of his workmanship. Even in our personal relationships, we often undervalue the beauty of loyalty and faithfulness. It is too easy for us to be offended and just move on to the next person. Perhaps we listen to someone else's gossip, form an opinion about a friend or family member, and simply walk away without any effort to seek understanding. Instead of counting relationship as cheap and easy to replace, loyalty communicates dedication, and that the relationship is valuable to you. This is why loyalty helps create trust equity, it communicates your dedication to the relationship. When you are loyal to the people in your life, you become trustworthy. When you are trustworthy, it builds confidence and reinforces the importance of being loyal. You grow in your own self-worth because you know you are trustworthy. Loyalty is one of the most important investments to build trust equity, and it strengthens your emotional growth. The following proverb illustrates the importance of loyalty and can help us see its value:

"Never let loyalty and kindness leave you! Tie them around your neck as a reminder. Write them deep within your heart; then you will find favour with both God and people and you will earn a good reputation." Proverbs 3:3-4 NLT www. thebible.com/116/pro3.3-4.nlt

There are a few keys in this proverb that can help us discover the value of loyalty and how to apply it to our relationships and see trust equity grow.

1. Loyalty and kindness – It's interesting that these two characteristics are tied together. I believe that it takes a great measure of kindness to be a loyal person. We all have many reasons to be offended by someone. But kindness is an internal choice. Kindness is not based on others' actions or attitudes, but on our own. When we choose kindness, it develops loyalty in us. It actually protects our heart from offence. My daughter Jélene said, "When there is an offence, we have already judged." She was sixteen when she said that to a group of people. And yes, I am a proud dad. Grace and kindness keep you from being offended because judgment can't enter your heart. You become trustworthy as a loyal person who doesn't quickly break relationship.

2. Display loyalty and kindness – Tying loyalty and kindness around our necks does three things. First, it actively puts it out there for everyone to see. It becomes a beautiful necklace that everyone can admire, which increases trust equity. Secondly, this necklace also allows your kids to witness what loyalty looks like. They experience it through you by watching you be loyal and kind to others. When loyalty and kindness is modelled, kids feel safe and they grow up with confidence. Its third benefit is to remind us of the value of loyalty and kindness when we may be tempted to give up on a relationship.

3. Write loyalty on your heart – When we engrave loyalty deep into our hearts, it becomes part of who we are and is offered unconditionally, which increases its value exponentially. It does not force someone to

love you; it invites them to. Loyalty becomes a value in our lives that drives the decisions we make. It ends up inviting loyalty from others. You reap what your heart has sown. It becomes an inspiration to those around you to be loyal as well.

4. You will find favour – People are attracted to kindness and loyalty. In my life, after my relational healing journey, I have often enjoyed favour from others. It has been a great blessing when people have gone out of their way to care for our family. I believe that this favour comes because loyalty and kindness have become strong values within my family. My children are all adults now, and they all still enjoy a tremendous amount of favour in their lives and are very loyal people.

5. A good reputation – Everyone wants a good reputation or to be trusted by others. Loyalty is a character trait that helps us earn a good reputation. because it shows we are trustworthy. When the people you relate to can depend on your faithfulness, your reputation is one of reliability. When we are loyal, it attracts loyal people into our lives. It is a slow, but sure, way to be known as a *trustworthy p*erson. People will develop relationship with you when they know they can trust you. It provides a fantastic sense of safety in your family and especially for your children. My children never had to worry that I would not be there for them.

Loyalty is truly a treasure that is often hidden in society today and certainly lost within relationships.

Fulfilling Promises

My last point on ways to build trust equity is to do what you promise to do. You have probably heard the saying, "Say what you mean; mean what you say." Breaking promises is one of the quickest ways to lose trust. When I was young, my dad was busy helping many people because he was a minister. In an effort to make me feel better, he would promise all kinds of things but then never follow through because something always came up. I hung on every one of my father's words, and it did make me feel better in the moment. However, as I got older, I didn't believe a word of those promises, and it led to a breach in relationship for many years. You read where that breach led me to at the beginning of this book. Thankfully we reconciled. He made things right; we were both able to forgive; and we had a great relationship for ten years before he passed away. Always keep your word, and you will invest in trust equity. When you follow through with even the smallest of commitments, you build trust, and the foundation of your home will become stronger. I always encourage people to under-promise and over-deliver. This habit will ensure there is lots of trust saved up in your bank.

If you have breached trust in some way, I encourage you to start rebuilding it today. You can do that by asking the ones you love if there is an area where you have let them down. Don't just let things go unspoken or unresolved. I have met many people who feel terrible for breaching trust but then feel too awkward to talk about it to the person. They just let it hang for years, assuming all is forgotten; but it's not. Take responsibility! Don't deflect or justify. Simply humble yourself, ask forgiveness, and make a new commitment to do better. Then, follow through and invite them to hold you accountable. This action will make a huge deposit into your trust bank. Remember *forgiveness is a gift, but trust is earned.* So, be prepared for the long haul it takes to earn that trust back. If your loved one has a difficult time trusting you, it does not mean they have not forgiven you. Leave no doubt in their minds by working hard and going above and beyond in fulfilling your promises, to keep depositing into their trust bank. It may take time and it can be frustrating to feel untrusted but keep depositing into the trust bank; get ridiculously rich in trust. Eventually you will earn their trust back.

Trust is the first foundational pillar to every healthy relationship because everything else flows from it, so it should be protected at all costs. One of the best ways to protect trust is by building the second pillar – Communication.

RELATIONSHIP CHALLENGE

1. Sit down with someone you're in relationship with and share something with them that you have never told them before. Provide insight into your heart.
2. If there is a promise you have made but have not followed through on, fulfill it this week.
3. Write a letter of apology to someone you were disloyal to, maybe a friend or an employer.
4. Show kindness to someone you have been rude to by sending a gift or a card with an apology and taking responsibility for your rudeness.

CHAPTER 2
PILLAR 2 – COMMUNICATION

One day when I was young, I was playing in the back yard. I was having fun goofing around and kicking a ball. I had been told not to kick the ball towards my mom's garden. Well, when you're in the world cup and you're about to score the winning goal to win the championship, you're not thinking about flowers. I gave a triumphant last kick imagining the winning goal hitting the back of the net while the crowd went crazy! The problem was that the ball didn't hit a net, but it sure did hit my mom's flower pots, and the noise was not the crowd but the pot breaking into a million pieces. I swung around to see if my mom was looking out the kitchen window, only to find her face looking at me with a certain look on it. You know the look, the one that sends terror into every fiber of your being. I didn't need to be told what was next; I knew what was coming.

My point is that communication is more than talking!

We communicate relational messages through many forms of communication including the silent treatment, body language and the way we behave towards a person. Communication can be one of the most difficult skills to learn and often affects all the other pillars. It's like a football offensive line, which has two functions: the first is to protect the quarterback, and the second is to create gaps for the running backs. Communication protects relationships and creates opportunity or spaces for them to grow or move forward. Communication has the power to create great relationships or completely destroy them. In my over thirty years of working with people, families, and organizations, miscommunication, or lack of communication, has done more harm than any other single thing. This is why it is a central pillar to a healthy foundation. The ability to express our hearts is vital to a healthy relationship. It goes beyond just saying words; it's communicating in a variety of ways that creates an emotional connection. This helps in relating to one another on a deeper level. When that kind of communication breaks down, we lose connection and stop communicating altogether. Often relationships focus on physical intimacy (the things we can see and touch) rather than emotional intimacy and heart connections (the things we can't see but feel emotionally). Both are important and often when we have the emotional connection, it enhances the physical interactions. There are some keys to better understand communication that will help you communicate more effectively.

VERBAL AND NON-VERBAL

When I kicked the soccer ball into my mom's flowerpot, her face expressed all I really needed to know. But communication is more than facial expression. Communication is a two-way interaction that involves both verbal and nonverbal expressions. It requires both sending and receiving messages. Very often, this is where a disconnect happens for people. For example, I may say one thing, but my wife hears something totally different. We were at Dairy Queen once on a date night, and I commented that I could not believe what they were charging for dipped cones nowadays! She got quiet for the rest of our time, and the date became as cold as the ice cream we were eating. When I asked her what was wrong, her answer was "NOTHING!" It took me weeks to figure out that what my wife heard was that she was not worth $2.50.

Although a funny story now, it was not so much then. Her silence was speaking louder than words could, but it did not help her communicate what she was feeling emotionally in a way that I could understand enough to help her feel better. I would spend any amount of money to make her happy but...well, you get the idea. Had she been able to just tell me and had I been more intuitive, we could have enjoyed the rest of our date. Things like crossed arms, turning our back to someone or giving the silent treatment are all saying something but are not communicating in a way that will help solve the problem. This causes a trust withdrawal that you may not even realize was made.

LISTEN TO UNDERSTAND

My daughter Jenna sighed with frustration once because when she shared a friendship problem with me, I went into *fix-it* mode. After all, her dad is a relationship specialist. She said, "Sometimes I don't want advice. I just want you to hear me." (That is, understand her heart.) Oops! We agreed that, from then on, she would let me know if she wanted my advice when venting.

What do I mean? Seek to know not only what is being said but why. In other words, seek understanding, not just information.

Have you ever had a conversation with someone and, although they are answering you, it's like they are somewhere else? We all have had those moments. It is important that when we are on the receiving end of communication, we try to seek not only what is being said but understanding what the other person is saying to us. There is a huge difference. Because communication is bidirectional, it is very important to understand what is being said and knowing why it is being said can really help you connect.

Often it is difficult for us to hear the why because the person may not even know why. They may be hurt and don't understand themselves why they are upset. But when we listen to understand, we can help to draw out what they are feeling. One way of gaining clarity is to ask questions, rather than making statements, until there is understanding. You can repeat back what you think they are saying to gain additional clarity. If you discover together what is going on, that builds connection and depth in the relationship.

SPEAK FROM THE HEART, NOT THE PAIN

One day when my son was young and I had just started my healing journey we were wrestling and he accidentally hurt me, I started yelling at him in anger as though he did it on purpose. I was quickly arrested by the big tears forming in his eyes and stopped myself, but the damage was done. Of course, I apologized, and we were able to talk through the event and forgive each other.

Often when we speak, our words reflect our pain or emotions rather than the deeper issues of the heart. You may be asking, what is the difference? The difference is this: speaking from our heart is speaking from a place of deep conviction within us. Speaking from our emotions is a reaction to an external circumstance that triggers an internal pain. We need to help others see what is going on in our hearts, so they understand where we are coming from. Often, people assume that the other person should just know or read our minds. This is an unspoken expectation that breaks down communication. You feel misunderstood, and they feel helpless. Simply being honest or transparent with where your heart is opens up communication.

Understanding how the brain works can help you know why we tend to communicate from our pain rather than our hearts. The primal part of the brain, which is located at the base of your skulls stores all the information we experience. It's like a CPU in a computer. It captures every second of our lives. When someone has hurt us, it even remembers the pain or emotion of that moment. So, when a similar experience is triggered by someone else your brain actually recalls the emotion you felt the first time. In other words, your brain takes you back in time and has you react out of pain from the past, rather than thinking it through and realizing it is a totally different situation. As soon as this reaction happens, your brain releases adrenaline into your blood stream and your whole body reacts. Have you ever overreacted to something and later felt silly and thought "Wow, why did I do that or say this?" You overreacted because your brain did not distinguish the time difference; it only remembered the emotion connected to the experience. So, when we have unresolved issues or pain from the past, situations we have not healed from, the emotions carry into the present-day relationships. In short, your communication is a reaction to pain rather than a response from your heart. It is okay to communicate that your heart was hurt, in fact, it is important to healing, but it is *how you say it* that communicates pain or heart.

BODY SPEAK

Your bodily position can say more than your words do at times. In fact, your physical bearing can actually communicate louder than words and even contradict what your words are saying. Your body tells people how interested you are in what they are saying or feeling. It tells people whether you're open to them or closed. Different body parts can say different things, but they all work in harmony to communicate a message whether you intend them to or not. Here are a few insights that may help you discern how you might be subconsciously communicating:

YOUR EYES

They are the windows to your soul. If your heart is open, they will be open and looking into the eyes of the other person. If you are lying, they will look up and away, or they will look down and away if you are disgusted or ashamed. Let your eyes convey compassion and openness. When you're hurt or experiencing shame, it is difficult to make eye contact and your avoidance conveys unintended communication. Looking openly into each other's eyes deepens connection and builds trust.

YOUR ARMS AND HANDS

Their position tells someone if you are open or closed. If they are crossed, you are closed, and if open, they invite dialogue. They can be used to reassure when they hug, to reject when they give someone the finger, or to promote violence when they push or throw something. Holding your hand up to someone to stop them from talking is saying, talk to the hand because I am not listening.

YOUR MOUTH

Words bring life or death depending on how they are used. When we complain, we erode connection, but when we affirm, we build confidence in the other person. It is important to communicate value, and we do that with words we speak. A gentle word turns away wrath. You also use your mouth to kiss someone. My kids use to call my dad's bald spot their kissing spot. They would jump up on his chair and climb around the back and kiss his head. They were communicating their affection for Grandpa. I hope my grandkids do that if I ever have a bald spot.

YOUR BACK

Many times, when we're angry, we simply walk away. By turning our back on someone, we are communicating that we don't value the other person enough to have their back. We are actually communicating rejection. When we face someone and express our hearts, even if that is painful, you communicate acceptance and an invitation to heal together.

Communication is a central pillar because it is essential to creating a culture of healthy relationships in every family or organization. Dr. James Dobson, a child psychologist did a study in which he discovered it takes seven positive words to negate one negative one. I shudder when I realize how many times that I've yelled at my kids out of frustration or anger through the years. Thankfully, I was always able to admit my mistake with my kids and ask for forgiveness. You can actually create the environment you desire with the words you speak. If you want a healthy culture in your relationships and your home, you have to use positive words to bring it into being, there is power in words. The next pillar will help you do this because it requires authenticity to communicate effectively.

RELATIONSHIP CHALLENGE

1. Work on making eye contact with the person you are speaking with and keep your body language in mind. Think about what you're communicating through your body language.
2. Sit down with someone important in your life and ask them questions about themselves, listen to understand how they are doing in that moment.
3. Make an appointment with someone you know you have miscommunicated with and share from your heart about what was going on in your heart when you miscommunicated. Explain why the miscommunication happened.

CHAPTER 3
PILLAR 3 – AUTHENTICITY

AUTHENTIC RELATIONSHIPS

When I was young, I never felt like I fit in because of the family pressures I previously mentioned. I learned to put on an act so people would like me. I remember when I was a teenager, I would make stories up to impress people, and when they found me out, I would get angry and defend myself. You see, I had not learned that being authentic would bring way more acceptance than being liked for who I was not. While helping a client navigate through a relational issue, I made this statement: "The key in every relationship is to BE YOURSELF. If you can't, then ask yourself why you can't." If I can't be myself with people I am in relationship with, there is something wrong either in my heart or theirs. It is likely both, but I can only change my own. In thinking about all this and asking those questions, I realized how much of our lives we spend trying to make people like us like I did. Insecurity and the desire to be accepted make us do all kinds of crazy things that just don't represent who we are. If someone doesn't like me for me, then is he really a friend? If people get to know the "fake me," do they only love the person I pretend to be? This becomes a real issue in family life because often, when we're dating, we are not ourselves as we try and win our now spouse's heart. However, once you live under the same roof, it is hard to keep the façade going. If kids don't think we are happy with them, they may act a certain way to gain approval. This behavior has real potential for them to sacrifice authenticity for favour. Imagine for moment that we actually invested the same amount of time and energy into being authentic in our relationships, strengthening them, investing in them, and enjoying them, as we do in being fake. It is actually more work being fake then it is to be authentic. If you did an inventory of your relationships and had to separate the real from the fake, how many friends would you have left? Personally, I would rather have one or two real, authentic relationships than a hundred shallow, fake ones. I would rather be unpopular and loved by a few than be popular with many at the cost of authenticity. Those who accept you for who you are and stick with you through everything are real friends.

During family coaching, it always amazes me how many secrets or deceptions exist between family members. Recently, I found out about a family secret. My aunt on my dad's side was adopted secretly, and I guess my grandparents had rescued her from a bad situation from another family member. They had decided that it would never be spoken of in the family again. I just do not understand how my family thought we would think any differently about her if we knew. I suppose it was in an era that looked down on having a child out of wedlock. However, it caused a whole family to be dishonest and inauthentic. It was potentially the seeds of shame that carried forward through the generations that caused me to be hurt by my parents trying to always look good to others. Being authentic creates a healthy, open culture in your family. Yes, there are moments we may hear something we don't want to, but by being real with each other, you have a chance to work through those moments. Authenticity develops transparency, and transparency creates intimacy.

So, how can you tell if someone is authentic?

AUTHENTIC PEOPLE AREN'T IN A HURRY

Relationships take time. Don't be in a hurry! Be at peace with who you are, and you will attract people who know who they are. People who are authentic will be patient in the process. They don't demand instant results. They are gracious in allowing you space and time to share your heart. These people don't let insecurity rush the process of building a relationship. My best friends are the longest relationships I have, including my wife and kids who are my best friends. I often tell parents that if they want to be a friend with their kids when they are adults, be their parent when they are young. That creates the opportunity for you to have friendship later when they have grown up.

AUTHENTIC PEOPLE ARE TRANSPARENT

If they can't be transparent, then they won't care what is going on inside of you. Authentic people know their weaknesses and will be honest about them. The word intimacy could be spelled 'into-me-you-see.' Authentic people have nothing to hide.

AUTHENTIC PEOPLE ARE ACTIVE LISTENERS

Authentic people genuinely care about what you have to say. They practice active listening to ensure they understand your heart more than the information you share. Active listening includes saying back to people what you think they said. You seek to understand their heart, not just the information. Active listeners are not self-focused but are attentive to those around them.

AUTHENTIC PEOPLE WEATHER THE STORMS

When trouble does come through misunderstandings, authentic people seek to make things right. They can apologize and take responsibility for their part. If someone maintains that any problem is always your fault, they are not being authentic. If you are blamed for everything, then the other person is deflecting their part because it is hard for them to admit their own failures. When you hide things in your own heart, it becomes difficult to see into another's heart.

AUTHENTIC PEOPLE SPEAK WELL OF OTHERS

If they talk trash about others *to you*, then chances are they will do the same *about you* to others. Authentic people are not insecure about you having other friends. They don't demand all your attention. They also do not use language that includes "always" or "never" as in "You never say this!" or "You always do that!" They understand that people make mistakes or forget, and their self-esteem is not determined by other peoples' mistakes. When someone speaks well about another, it is an indicator that they live out of their heart. They believe the best of others because they are secure in themselves and consequently, they can be authentic.

Remember that by being authentic you will attract authentic people!

You may be asking where do I start? Or what fosters authenticity in family?

I often tell people that self-awareness brings choice. As a result, self-awareness is critical to develop authenticity, in other words being able to know yourself. When you *know yourself*, the outcome is you are able to *be yourself.*

KNOWING YOURSELF

Self-esteem

Self-esteem is how you feel about yourself. If you don't feel good about who you are, it is impossible to feel good about others, and this prevents us from being authentic. Feeling good about yourself is not pride. It is, in fact, humility. It is accepting your victories and failures as growth opportunities, not measurements of your value. I believe your value comes from God and not from other people's opinions of you. True self-esteem is being grateful and embracing who God made you to be. Your value is not determined by other people's inability to see it. When you feel esteemed you will esteem others.

Self-image

Self-image is how you see yourself. Similar to self-esteem, if you don't see yourself in the right light, you can't see others in the right way either. Often if we have a warped view of ourselves, that becomes the filter or lens through which we see other people, and we judge them accordingly. For example, if I don't trust myself to make good decisions, I won't believe anyone else can either. This steals authenticity because we don't see anyone as trustworthy, and we start to hide behind a façade. We put walls around our heart. How you view yourself impacts how you view everything, including authenticity. I have had people actually tell me that they think being authentic is a weakness. They don't see that being authentic requires humility, and that takes great strength.

Self-dignity

Self-dignity is how you treat yourself. When you don't feel good or see yourself in the right light, you begin to treat yourself badly. Treating oneself badly can take many forms, however the root of it is a belief that you don't deserve to be treated nicely or have good things happen to you. Addiction, self-harm, and other behaviors put you in harm's way of being even more hurt. The problem also spreads to our relationships because when you can't treat yourself with dignity you won't treat others with dignity either. It is hurtful for a loved one to watch you self-destruct and harm yourself and them.

Dignity is respecting people, including respecting them with your words and actions. Respecting yourself is part of the value of dignity. How is your self-talk stealing dignity from you? Are you willing to change your narrative? What behaviors do you have that steal dignity from you and others? What actions could you take to build dignity in your family? I often tell parents that when they correct their children, they must separate the child's personhood from the behavior, so the parent doesn't rob the child of dignity. For example, if a child is mean to their siblings, don't call the child mean. Instead say, "You're a kind person, so why were you acting that way to your brother?" Stealing dignity erodes trust and takes a toll on relationships. The world has not always modelled dignity, but we can! With dignity being in the core of who you are, you will inspire others to be people of dignity too.

Being Yourself

A natural outflow of knowing yourself is to be yourself. When I learned to just be myself, I began to gain confidence, and as I gained confidence, I began to treat myself better and expected others to do the same. The more I accepted my mistakes as learning opportunities, the less I felt the need to cover them. In fact, I have learned to take them to someone and open up about them so that I can live free. Being myself has allowed me to be more open and transparent. The risk in that is I can get hurt; however, a by-product of the confidence I gained was that I am learning to set clear boundaries (that is an ongoing learning). Healthy boundaries protect the environment in a family. At times, you may actually view boundaries as rejection or as not getting your own way, so you don't respect them. When the boundaries are not respected, you put walls up that then create an environment of self-protection, that, in turn, creates an environment of secrecy and robs us of authenticity. In his book *Boundaries*, Dr. Henry Cloud uses the illustration of a house with a front yard. The yard has a low fence with a gate. As you build relationship with someone and that person builds trust equity with you by respecting the boundary, you can invite him or her into the yard. As the trust and respect grows, you may invite them into the house. Then you are free to enjoy each other's companionship. In the same way, when families have not had healthy boundaries you need to begin with small steps. Some family members may need to go back outside the gates and relearn each other's boundaries. This requires everyone getting real with each other. It requires being authentic because each person needs to be real in order to communicate and respect each other's boundaries.

As you can see, authenticity is central to a healthy relationship and culture within a family. It builds trust equity and open communication, allowing everyone to be real with themselves and open with one another. When lived out, authenticity leads us to the next pillar – honesty because it allows us to be honest.

RELATIONSHIP CHALLENGE

1. Do a heart check; ask yourself if you're being authentic? Make a list of ways you hide who you really are. Challenge yourself to get real. Then, meet with a trusted friend and confess what you have been hiding.

2. Ask five trusted people in your life to tell you what they see in you. Ask what traits or character points they appreciate about you. What do they like about you? Affirmation builds self-worth, so it's important to do this with an open mind and heart. It also can show you areas that you need to work on.

3. Think back to your childhood and identify where your belief about yourself started. If it is a negative point that affects your self-worth, challenge that belief by asking yourself, "Did I choose that belief, or was it imposed on me?" Challenge the negative belief about who you are.

CHAPTER 4
PILLAR 4 – HONESTY

There is an old saying: "What they don't know, won't hurt them." Not true! It will hurt your trust equity, break down communication, and cause you to be disingenuous. In short, the first three pillars get wiped out if honesty is not in place. Dishonesty has tangible, negative effects on your relationships. It's best to come clean and work through things together. This action will actually deepen your relationship. As I coach people, I find that dishonesty is one of the biggest factors when trust is broken. On the flip side, honesty is a great source of healing. When someone is honest, it creates an atmosphere of transparency and trust. Dishonestly is not just a matter of lying, it is also omitting information. Hiding something from someone is a subtle dishonesty that erodes a relationship from the inside out. For example, if my wife did something that hurt my feelings and I don't tell her because perhaps I am scared of her reaction, I never clear my heart, and eventually resentment begins to grow. A few years ago, Sandi and I lost everything in a fire that burned our condo building down. It was a very difficult thing to go through, but I always look for the blessings in disasters. As I conveyed the story to people, I always ended up saying something along the line that at least no one was hurt. I didn't realize that every time I said this and other positive things, my wife was boiling in her heart. It hurt her every time, but she didn't say a thing to me. Over time she built up resentment towards me but didn't say anything. Feeling the tension, I asked what was wrong and got 'nothing,' which was dishonest. Finally, on a holiday to recoup from the whole thing, she, all of a sudden, started unloading all her resentment all at once. I felt attacked and didn't know what to do. I had made her feel that she could not grieve the loss of so many memories; what I had been saying made her feel guilty for being sad about the loss of everything. I had no idea because she didn't say anything; however, thankfully, we were then able to talk it through, and everything was OK between us. Resentment can be a relationship killer that few can survive. When we are compelled to lie, including omissions, to those we love, it fractures the relationship at a core level because it undermines the other pillars. It literally creates an unstable foundation.

You now know that dishonesty can have negative consequences, so why are you dishonest at times? Dishonesty can stem from a number of roots – fear, shame, or selfishness – to name the few, the following is a list of some reasons why you may choose dishonestly.

FEAR OF REACTION

When my son was in his later teen years, he went through a phase of lying about things, mostly things surrounding achievements or being concerned that he would somehow disappoint me. Of course, I found out, and he was super embarrassed. But his fear of my reaction was what kept him doing it. I am grateful that we worked through that season together, and I could reassure him of my love and how proud I am of him. Today, we enjoy being best friends. Often, you assume how someone may react to what you have to tell him or her, so you may withhold information or outright lie about something you did or said. When the assumption is based on previous experience or a partial truth, the damage can be taken to a whole new level. In fact, you can actually get angry over what you assume another person might say or do and actually withhold truth as punishment. In my experience, most relational breakdowns happen based on assumptions and partial truths. It has been said that assumption is the enemy of faith. It is hard to have faith in someone when we make assumptions about them. I have a saying that sheds some light on the power of assumption. *Perception is reality, but it is not always actuality.* What I mean by this saying is, sometimes your perception is very real to you, but your perception is not necessarily the actual truth. Fear is often at the root of your perceptions being wrong. FEAR stands for *False Evidence Appearing Real.* Fear can drive you to dishonesty. It can be fear of rejection or fear of failure, or even fear of abandonment. Dishonesty is actually often a low self-esteem problem. To overcome this root issue, you need love because love dispels fear. From love, work at building confidence, knowing that even if you make a mistake, that mistake does not define you. Contrast your identity with your behavior and choose to make the changes, so you can be honest. In my son's case, I was able to say to him, "You are not a liar, so why are you lying to me?" I was able to contrast his personhood with his behavior. Honesty is a powerful value that will strengthen your relationships and protect your heart.

SHAME

Guilt acknowledges that "you did something wrong" and leads you to apologize and make it right. But shame affirms that "you are something wrong" and often cripples you from taking responsibility. Often when you believe that "I am something wrong," the belief prevents you from being honest. As a result of shame, when you do something wrong, you know it is wrong, but have the need to cover it up. You don't want anyone to find out, especially your loved ones. When you cover it up over and over, you will eventually develop a shame complex. When you allow guilt to go unchecked, it becomes shame. Once that happens, we begin to add layers to dishonestly. In fact, dishonestly can grow to the point that you deceive yourself. This warped view of yourselves gets to the point that you actually get angry when you are challenged. Shame actually comes from wounds that were inflicted when you were little, and at that time, they begin to create a negative self-image. You believe lies about yourself based on what you were told as kids. The way to overcome shame is to know the truth about yourself and about your value, then you can construct a proper view of yourself. One thing that can help is by understanding that your strengths and weaknesses are equals, because they are both opportunities to grow in character. As I said earlier self-awareness gives you choice, so when you can admit your mistakes and take ownership you can take corrective action to grow your character. People say that trials can show you a person's character, however I have often said I believe trials reveal character, so I know what to work on. Everyone has weaknesses, but they don't define you. What you chose to do about them will better define you but always remember it is God that gives you your value. In the same way, your strengths don't define you. They are given to you to fulfill your purpose in life and to do the best you can with what you have. So, if you give emotional energy to either strengths or weakness, you will feel they measure your value. In other words, the truth will set you free. The truth is that you have value, and your mistakes don't change that. When you make a mistake, simply be honest about it and then it does not erode your value.

WANTING YOUR OWN WAY

Dishonesty can also be as simple as wanting your own way. I believe that the opposite of love is not hate, it is selfishness. When you become so self-focused that you lie to get your own way, it will destroy your relationships. I often tell couples that they can be right and wrong at the same time. What I mean is that they can be right about an issue or facts but have a wrong attitude or a self-centered approach concerning that particular issue. Rebellion, or always wanting your own way, forces you to be dishonest to ensure you get what you want. Wanting your own way causes you to treat others and yourself badly and to be dishonest. The way to overcome this attitude is to humble yourself. Rick Warren, in his book, Purpose Driven Life – What on earth am I here for; said humility is not thinking less of yourself, it is thinking of yourself less.

The second way is to put others first and let go of entitlement. Entitlement is when you think you deserve something that you have not worked for. It can be very subtle, but it is when you expect to get something from someone without ever telling him or her what you want. I once had a boss that seemed to just dislike me from the very beginning. I was already working for the organization and had had success at what I did. I never told anyone that I might be interested in advancement, and when this guy was hired as my boss, I said I didn't care (a Lie). But I did care and was mad. I felt a little ripped off and devalued. I came to realize that I had pride in my heart and felt entitlement, thinking I deserved the job more than him. I humbled myself and carried on doing the best job I could. When we do humble ourselves, we can be honest, which builds trust equity. A short time later a leadership opportunity presented itself to me and I have never looked back.

Lies erode trust and hurt intimacy within relationships, and as mentioned, omission is a form of lying. Honesty is a central pillar, it undergirds truth and helps to build authentic, healthy relationships that flourish when hard times come. Society has lost the art of honestly, but I think it is that they simply don't see the damage it does to themselves and the people around them.

This leads to the last pillar because honesty invites honour

RELATIONSHIP CHALLENGE

1. What lies have you told lately? Go to someone you lied to even a little white lie and confess that you lied and ask for forgiveness.
2. Tell someone what you fear and tell them how you hide it. This action is not an easy thing to do, but it sure is freeing.
3. Do something this week to put other first. Humble yourself and do something that is out of your comfort zone to bless someone else.

CHAPTER 5
PILLAR 5 – HONOUR

Honour is another one of those lost arts in today's society. In an age of attack politics, cyberbullying, public ridicule, and social media exposure, honour does not seem to be modelled anymore. There is something that is built into every human that ties their value to their family of origin. More to the point, how we see our family effects how we see ourselves. If we cannot find something to honour in them, we will be unable to honour ourselves. Honour is closely tied to your value because it comes from your hearts. How you treat others displays how much value you place on them and yourself. A close friend, Jack Toth, who I worked with at Impact Society and who developed some of the principles shared in this book, was once teaching a 'Heroes' class of eighth graders, and there was a girl in the class, I will call Sue. Sue had a reputation with the boys that she was easy because of the way she dressed. She was seeking attention and got a lot of it by the way she dressed and flirting. It did not seem like she valued herself. When Jack was teaching the class about honouring your parents, she got upset. He encouraged the class that if it was difficult to honour their parents to find someone in their bloodline they could. She shot her hand up and said she had no one to honour. "My whole family are drug addicts and welfare bums," she said. He went through a few ideas with her like uncles, cousins, or great grandpa, but she said she had no one. She seemed dejected, and he was at a loss as to what to say to her. A few classes later, she came bouncing into class. She ran straight to Jack, "I thought of someone!"

He asked, "You thought of whom?" He wasn't thinking about the previous class. She said, "I found out that I have an aunt in Seattle that is a nurse, and nurses help people, right"? He agreed that they do. She said, "So, I can honour her"? Jack responded, "You sure can!" This girl came into the very next class dressed appropriately, and as the semester went by, she went from a failing grade to honour roll. WHY? The principal Jack was teaching is when you find someone in your bloodline to honour, you begin to see honour in yourself and then you can see your value in a new way. By the way, my friend Jack never ever said anything about the way she dressed or tried to correct her behavior. He simply showed her that she had value. We must model honour to the next generation. You can't always honour one's behavior, but you can honour one's personhood. Kids will take your cues, and if you are not honouring others, they may not honour you.

So, what is Honour? It is a *lifting up* of another by respecting them.

Honour prefers others, it is what you think of them. You honour people that you think highly of, and you often put them ahead of your own desires. For example, you would go out of your way to serve someone you honour and respect.

Honour elevates others, it is how you speak of them. When you honour someone, you speak highly of him or her to others. You brag about how awesome they are. You point out their good qualities and build them up with words and actions.

Honour celebrates others, it is how you treat them. When you honour someone, you celebrate their accomplishments and treat them with respect. Honour is not jealous, and it does not compete.

Honouring someone is simply treating them with respect and encouraging others to do the same. Honour is a condition of your heart and an internal value. You choose to honour because of who you are, not because someone has earned it. An example of this is that you are to honour authority. Honouring the title or position someone has, such as a teacher or a police officer. When you honour those in authority, you teach your kids to honour you. If my wife has done something to hurt me emotionally, I still choose to honour her because she is my wife.

Often, I hear parents dishonouring each other or someone in author- ity while the kids are listening in. Later, those same parents say to me, "I just don't understand why they don't respect me?" In short *you get what you model*. I have chosen honour to be one of the highest values and virtues in my life. This has not been easy; however, it is now woven into the fabric of my character because it is part of who I am. I practiced it so much that it has become part of my nature. This has helped me treat people with respect. Choosing to honour brought a kindness out of me that I didn't know was there. It helped me treat people that served me with gratitude and honour. In short, it changed my attitude so much that I believe it made a way for me to help the many people I get the privilege of serving every day. I have had the honour of officiating many funerals in my thirty years of doing this and it always impacts me when people give tributes to the deceased. Person after person gets up to honour them and I can't help but wonder why we don't do that more while they are alive. Imagine with me having an honour night at your home. You have a meal together and then each person takes a turn and speaks highly of each other. You each say why you honour the others. It would change the whole dynamic of your family life. Recently, I had the opportunity to be involved in a training week. The final night as we sat around a large table with 25 people, each person took a turn to honour someone at the table. To say something good they saw in them through the week. I was blown away by the power of that exercise. There were many healing tears and lots of joy being experienced through the whole time.

RELATIONSHIP CHALLENGE

1. Find someone in your family and honour them publicly, tell the world why you honour them. Plan a honour themed dinner with your family and take turns honouring each other.
2. Find someone you admire and celebrate his or her achievements. You could have a plaque made or give them a gift card, then tell them you wanted to celebrate them.
3. Think of someone you may have dishonoured and go and apologize for doing so. Then, honour them.

SECTION 1 SUMMARY

In this section, we have learned how important it is to have a healthy foundation for every relationship to build a healthy relational culture in your home or organization. These five pillars will help you live a full life, rich with relationships in your family, friendships and co-workers.

The next section will be focused on building a strong framework. Having a framework keeps us moving in the right direction and keeps you on the same page with others. Although this section is focused on family life, it can apply to organizations as well, especially if it is used as a relational model.

SECTION 2
BUILDING A STRONG FRAMEWORK

In this section, we will begin build on the foundation we have laid. In our metaphor of having a well-built house, once a heathy foundation has been established you begin to frame out the house. Framing defines the spaces and describes what each room will be used for. In the same way in a family, you want to provide a framework of how you will relate to each other. The relationship framing defines how you will interact, what is important and show you where you are going as a family. It puts boundaries in place that will let everyone know how they can contribute to the culture of the home.

CREATING A HEALTHY FAMILY CULTURE

After a healthy foundation of trust, communication, authenticity, honesty, and honour has been established in your relationships, it is time to begin building the framework, which creates the family culture.

One Christmas when I was young, our family gathered for the holidays. Because I am the youngest by eight years, all of my adult siblings came with their families. As was often the case, it did not take long for our family gathering to begin to deteriorate into dysfunction. Arguments broke out and escalated into physical fights between brothers. Even though we grew up in a very structured home, it was a structure of discipline and rules, not agreement and connection. It always ended with mom crying and dad yelling, trying to get control of it all. Please understand that my family loves each other. They just had a difficult time focusing on a healthy foundation, nor did we have a framework for relating to each other in place. In this second section of the book, I am going to provide you with a framework that you can anchor to the foundation.

CHAPTER 6
FOUR PARTS OF THE FRAMEWORK

There are four parts to a framework, each of which helps a family to move in the same direction while creating a healthy relational culture.

1. Vision – is what you want to build.
2. Mission – is how you will build it.
3. Purpose – is why you're building.
4. Values – are the materials you build with.

These four areas, when done well and with agreement, help a family or organization grow together. A family that grows together, stays together. Every family needs to have common goals so they can link arms with one another. A unified vision and mission that is developed by a family that knows their purpose (why they are a family) will create strong values.

The more unified the family is, the stronger the framework will be. The result is living out the five pillars of the foundation. Including everyone in this framing process achieves the unity I speak of. The more each person has input the better the outcome, the stronger the framework is.

To use another analogy to help show the value of the framework let's look at the corporate world for a moment. In the corporate world, vision and mission statements provide riverbanks that keep companies moving in the right direction. These statements help organizations reach their goals. I believe these statements can do the same for families. As I work with people on relationship matters in my coaching practice, I have discovered one thing that they all have in common. None of them have vision and mission statements for their families. This practice just has not been taught in the family context.

Perhaps it sounds crazy at first, but vision and mission statements can have tremendous value for families. They create a *pulling together* motion rather than a *drifting apart* response.

What helps create the flow of a family in the first place is to know your purpose. Using a water illustration, to live without purpose is like climbing into a dingy and being set adrift on an ocean. The current of life's circumstances will take you and your family wherever the current goes. You will simply drift from here to there and may ultimately drift apart. It is important to know, that the move from drifting on an ocean, to flowing in a river comes from understanding why you are a family and setting the riverbanks in place. To know your purpose moves you from individual goals to united group goals. This means you work for *we* rather than *me*.

I was called to work with a family whose son was having full blackout temper tantrums. This wonderful little guy just could not regulate his emotions. He was struggling at school as well, so I was asked to work with him. As I began to work with the family, I could see that they were not working together, but against each other. This eight-year-old was caught in the middle of all the tension and did not know how to process it all emotionally. He would have a temper tantrum to try and deal with it all and to pull the attention toward him in the hope that this strategy would stop his parents from fighting.

I took this family through the process of developing a vision statement, mission statement, and set of values. The kids worked on it with mom and dad. In the end, they all came to an agreement about what kind of family they wanted to be and how they were going to treat each other to get there. They made riverbanks out of their vision and mission statements, so they could flow in the same direction. They put it all together on a poster that the kids made and hung it on the wall in the dining room, so they could read it at every dinnertime.

One particularly bad day, mom and dad were arguing. This eight-year-old, without a word, walked over, took their hands, and walked the parents over to the poster, pointed at it, and walked away. Mom and dad knew exactly what he was saying and started laughing. Of course, this changed the mood in the whole house. He had very few meltdowns from that day forward.

To fully understand the power of vision and mission statements, we need to define them. Successful leaders, by means of carefully chosen, inspiring words, convey the direction of their organization. Similarly, by crafting clear mission and vision statements, you can powerfully communicate your intentions and motivate your team, family, or organization to have a common vision for the future.

FAMILY VISION STATEMENT

While the idea of developing a family vision statement might seem, at first, a bit outlandish, the work investment can provide insight into the future and a clarity for the members of your family. A vision statement can give hope for tomorrow and guidance for today, providing a map to help avoid chaos. This intentional investment in your combined future increases your chance of successful family life exponentially.

Webster's definition of Vision
Vision: the act or power of anticipating that which will or may come to be.

A Vision Statement helps the Person or Family see the future!
If you google companies vision statements, it will give you good examples of how they may help you. A few good ones I found are:

Amazon – "Our vision is to be earth's most customer-centric company; to build a place where people can come to find and discover anything they might want to buy online."

Nike – "To bring inspiration and innovation to every athlete in the world."

Starbucks – "to establish Starbucks as the premier purveyor of the finest coffee in the world while maintaining our uncompromising principles while we grow."

By now you may be saying, "Mark, what is yours?" I'm glad you asked!

The Gordon Family's vision statement is: "To reveal the value every person possesses and the value of God to every person." This statement has kept our family in a positive place. Many times, when my kids were young, I would ask if how they were acting towards their sibling or mom at that moment was showing them how valuable they are. Our vision helped remind us that no matter what was going on we could still treat each other as valuable. Even though now as adults they may not remember the statement itself the fruit of keeping this vision active throughout their childhood is that now, when they are all adults, they are good friends. We have a great time together whenever we gather. You may wonder how to build a vision statement. The following page has a step by step process to help you, it is hard work but I know you can do it!

VISION CHALLENGE

A Five-Step Plan for Building a Vision Statement

1. *Pick a hero.*
   The idea is to pick someone you admire. Someone you would want to spend a day with asking questions, It can be real or fictional, dead or alive. What about them makes you want to invest the time? What would you ask them?

2. *Identify what you like about your hero.*
   This analysis will reveal to you the traits that you value and why they are important to you. Which of their traits impresses you most?

3. *Write a list of the traits*
   You can use a white board, flip chart, or electronically. Have each person in the family contribute to the list.

4. *Circle the traits that most describe your heart*
   If you are doing the exercise with family, look at words or sentences you all share and start there.

5. *Build a sentence*
   After circling all the words, build a sentence out of them. Use your imagination to visualize what kind of person or family that you want to be and simply using the words collected for the sentence. (Include your kids in this process if age appropriate).

The sentence should be a general statement of what you want to achieve as a family. For example, if you picked a superhero who helps others, like Superman, take the traits you admire and make a sentence, your vision statement might look like this: "We are a family who shows kindness to each other and helps others do the same."

Your Vision Statement is:

Congratulations! You now have one of the riverbanks that will get your family flowing in the same direction! Now, let's build the other one.

CHAPTER 7
FAMILY MISSION STATEMENT

A family mission keeps the family pulling together, so family members achieve the outcome they desire. A mission adds purpose to family life and defines the journey you are on together. When my kids were young our journey together shifted from living life by accident to living on mission. I felt a call to empower others, and to begin passing on the blessings I had received in my healing journey. The family all agreed and shared that sense of calling on the whole family. We took a huge leap of faith to start a non-profit organization to help youth. This gave our whole family a strong sense of mission together and shaped who we were as a family. I remember when we started taking foster kids in, we felt to focus on teenagers as that was our main focus. This one young man came to live with us for a season. He was a strong bulky guy who had a very difficult life and at the time was kicked out of his home. He had developed a very hard heart to survive all he had endured. He was quiet but you could feel the anger just under the surface and it would explode in violence with his peers. At first, Sandi and I were not sure about having him come and stay with us because we wanted to keep our own kids safe. However, our hearts were broken for this young man and so we sat down with our kids and talked about it. We explained that this young man had some pain in his heart and that he may be frustrated sometimes and that they could come to us whenever they were concerned. Now before you ask, let me answer your question, we always kept our kids safe and had many protocols to ensure they were. Also, we the adults made the final decision however we believe that as a family we are on mission together and so every voice should be heard, especially when those decisions can affect the whole family. We always have done this even to this day. Back to my story, our youngest at the time was too young to express her thoughts in any detail about things as she was 3 at the time. However, when this young man came into the house on the first day, I could tell he was super nervous and apprehensive. I showed him his room then brought him into the living room to meet the family. He was sitting on the couch when Jenna came flying around the corner and did a six-foot leap onto his knee. She looked at him right in the face and said "Hi my name is Jenna, what is yours, you will be loved here" jumped down and ran off to play. I looked at this young man, who was hardened by life, melt into a puddle of smiles and tears rolling down his cheeks. Now that is a family on mission!!

Being on mission together forges a healthy culture within the family that few other things can. I didn't have to tell Jenna to make him feel loved and welcome she instinctively knew what to do. My kids all had and have an amazing capacity to serve others and to express love to them.

Webster's definition of Mission: the business with which a group is charged.

Whereas a vision says *what* you want to do; a mission is *how* you will carry it out.

How our family lives out our vision is through the mission. The Gordon family mission statement is:

"We are committed to making a difference in the world by cultivating healthy relationships and being a loving family who serves our community with honour and integrity."

Vision and mission statements guide our decision-making and keep us pulling together, toward making a difference. When we struggle in our relationships, or find ourselves in difficult circumstances, we revisit these statements and then make the decision to live them out.

This worked very dramatically a few years ago. There was some tension between my wife and I, and by *some*, I mean a lot! It was affecting our home life. Our youngest daughter had finally had enough and called her married siblings to do an intervention. They sat mom and dad down and reminded us what kind of family we were and that our actions were not lining up with our family's mission. To say the least, our children's mediation got our attention.

It was after that intervention that my wife and I sat down and were able to get to the root of the tension. I am so grateful that my kids have the freedom to hold us accountable to the vision and mission that guide us as a family. It is important to note that they did not quote the vision or mission statement, they have become such a part of our lives that they are simply woven into the fabric of our family. It takes time and effort; our family did not arrive at this point by accident. It takes intentionality, agreement and a lot of grace to develop a healthy relational culture in a family but it helps to know how you are going to get there. A mission statement is a daily reminder to the family of who they are and where they are going.

Building a mission statement is similar to creating the vision statement. However, you build the mission statement with the vision in mind. Remember, the mission statement describes how you will live out your vision, so it is a bit more detailed. Just ensure that you don't make it too long to remember it easily.

MISSION STATEMENT CHALLENGE

Four steps to building a mission statement

1. Looking at your vision statement from chapter 6, discuss how you would accomplish that vision. Write down highlights that stand out in short phrases.
2. List the top three goals you would like your family to accomplish in the next thirty years. These goals should be relational or accomplishment goals.
3. What is the one thing you would like your family to be known for? When people talk about your family what would you like them to say?
4. Using all the words and phrases from this exercise form a sentence that describes your mission. This is typically a little longer than your vision statement.

For example, remember the Gordon family vision statement, "To reveal the value every person possesses and the value of God to every person."

To live this out our mission statement is "We are committed to making a difference in the world by cultivating healthy relationships and being a loving family who serves our community with honour and integrity."

You can see that the vision statement is about who you are, and the mission statement is how you will carry that identity out.

Your Mission Statement is...

Congratulations! You have now built the second riverbank! Now, let's open the dam and let the river run.

CHAPTER 8
FAMILY PURPOSE

If a vision is *what* and mission is the *how*, then the purpose is the *why!* Simon Sinek's famous "Know your why!" TED talk underlines the importance of knowing why you are doing something is a powerful tool to accomplish it. Living by accident gives to much room for life's storms to alter the course of your relationships. Today, the divorce rate is at an all-time high. The result is a crisis in society, families are being torn apart and kids are having to navigate living in multiple homes with new people coming in and out of their young lives. It has created an instability in family and society as a whole. I have worked with thousands of people in relationship crisis and much of it can be traced back to insecurity and the results of family of origin turmoil. When Sandi and I met, I had addiction issues, however they were the symptom of something far deeper. I had grown up believing I was an accident, that my very existence caused trouble for my family. As a result, I never believed I had a purpose, I did not know *why* I was born. Sandi had her own issues that affected her ability to understand her purpose. The first years of our marriage her very difficult and lead to a time where we were separated and living a thousand kilometers apart. I had no idea what was to come. I knew I wanted to save my family but also knew Sandi was done with my addictions. In that time, I was very broken, I was at the end of myself, this is when I came to faith in God. Right away, I felt an overwhelming sense that I was created for a purpose, that I was on this earth for a reason. The first thing I did was to call Sandi and tell her that I believed a new life was about to happen. As I shared my encounter with God's love she began to weep on the other end of the phone. I asked her why she was crying, and she told me that she had had the same experience with God and she also came to faith that very morning. Here we were a thousand kilometers apart and experienced the same thing the same morning, to say it changed our lives would be a gross understatement, it transformed our lives and our marriage. We now had a purpose, we know right away that our family was going on a healing journey, it took a few more years to realize that our calling, our purpose, our *WHY* is to help others heal too. Our purpose together has shaped our lives and we have been living out our *why* ever since.

A family, that knows why they exist, grows together rather than apart. They link arms to fulfill their purpose! If vision and mission are the riverbanks that allow the purpose to flow. Purpose and values are the water that keeps the family moving and growing together.

So, "How do you know your why?"

At times, it is good to look back, so you can move forward. There are clues throughout your life that point you in the direction of your purpose. Things you love to do, things you dream about achieving can all be pointers. Your gifts and abilities also point you in the right direction. It amazes me to see how aligned my passion, gifts and personality are. In my wife's case, the same thing, what she loves to do and how good she is at it align with her purpose. I realized that we were very different people and have very different gifts. I am visionary and not very organized; however, Sandi is highly organized and has an amazing ability to get things done. Although we are very opposite, we carry the same heart to help others, I do it with inspiration and encouragement she does it by helping organize their lives. I can't do what she does, and she can't do what I do, but together we are a great team. We live out our purpose together by honoring and respecting each other's contribution to the family and mission. Family unity is often confused as uniformity, the fact is everyone in your family will have both individual and family purpose. Each person has unique personalities, gifts and passions, the art is to harmonize them into a family focus without taking away from individual uniqueness. You do that, by honoring one another and appreciating their unique contribution.

Remember when you first fell in love with your spouse? Which personality traits did you love about your partner? What was it that made you commit to a life together? Think back to when you looked at your child for the first time. What did you feel? The first time I looked at my first born something shifted in my heart. I cannot explain what I felt like, but it was the first moment I had a glimpse of unconditioned love. Something inside me knew that there was more to life than what I had experienced. I now had a huge responsibility to give my kid a better life then I had lived. The simple answer is LOVE. Love brought you together, and it is love that will keep you together. That is a powerful *why*. However, remember that love is a choice, not just a feeling alone. We may feel love at the beginning, but we must choose every day to express that love. I had to learn to invest in the love I felt by making selfless choices to grow and define it, so my family not only heard me say I loved them, but they experienced the love I have for them. In the famous bible verse about love in 1 Corinthians 13:4 it provides a description what love in action looks like. "Love is patient and kind. Love is not jealous or boastful or proud or rude. It does not demand its own way. It is not irritable, and it keeps no record of being wronged. It does not rejoice about injustice but rejoices whenever the truth wins out. Love never gives up, never loses faith, is always hopeful, and endures through every circumstance." New Living Translation. WOW imagine a family that lives on purpose with love fueling their decisions.

What did you dream about together when you first met? I remember my kids coming home after spending time with their, now spouses, and sharing the conversations they had about the life they are dreaming about together.

Go back and reflect on your journey together. In that time of reflection, you will find clues that can help you articulate your why. This process is hard work and takes a lot of thought and dialogue, but it is so important. The *why* or your purpose is not so much a statement as it is a deep conviction in your heart. Just know that it adds fuel to the vision and mission. By the way, the vision and mission will also point to your purpose! When I met Sandi, we did not have any thoughts like these, and we drifted. We relied on feelings and emotions but did not understand companionship or living on purpose. As mentioned in this chapter, it was when we began to discover that we wanted to spend our lives *in the service of others* that the why became clear. After thirty-seven years of marriage, at the time of writing this book, I can tell you that our love is deeper than ever, and our why is stronger than it has ever been. We are determined to finish our journey strong. And now that we have grandchildren, we are even more purposeful about passing on a legacy of service to our family.

Everyone has a purpose, there are no exceptions, regardless of your experiences in life and the pain that came from them, you can live out your purpose. However, it takes intentionality and hard work, regardless of where you started you can finish well.

FAMILY PURPOSE CHALLENGE

Plan a family meeting, and read this chapter to the family, discuss each person's passions, gifts and personalities. Talk about what you could do as a family together that would impact the world and write your answers on a white board or flip chart. Talk through the questions in the previous paragraphs individually and then bring them together; you will discover your *why* where they intersect. Now you can make a commitment to live this out as your purpose. I even suggest that you make a contract based on your vision, mission, and purpose, then sign it, frame it, and hang it on the wall. Make it a family art project, you could then have it placed in a prominent place in your home.

CHAPTER 9
FAMILY VALUES

Values are a set of virtues that are very important to you. Also referred to as guiding principles, they help give us a moral compass that direct our life decisions. In a real way they are the very things you value in your life most. You can have many or a just a few, but they all effect the way you live. For this reason, it is important to know what they are, so you can intentionally communicate your family values in how you speak to and treat each other. I recommend having between three to five that are easily remembered. Values are the guiding principles for your family purpose. Coming back to our original illustration of a well-build house. The values are the nails that anchor the framework in place. They are the glue that holds the family together, they keep us safe in the storms of life and protect the heart of the family. One of my highest values is honour, it helps me live out my purpose in serving others because it has placed a high value on how I see and treat people. This was experienced one time when a server in a restaurant was providing very poor service. Before my healing journey, and adopting values in my life, I would have treated this server poorly and got her in trouble with her supervisor. On this day, I chose to live out my value of honour and treated her with respect and asked her if she was ok? She broke down crying and explained that she was going through a very difficult time in her life. I said a few encouraging things and told her how valuable she was and then gave her a very large tip. She came running out as I walked towards my car and hugged me and thanked me. She said I had no idea what it meant to her that someone treated her with respect and cared enough to ask if she was ok. I imagine her service improved that day as a result of this encounter. One thing I have discovered, is that all behavior has a cause and effect that proceeded it. Whenever I find someone with a bad attitude, or poor service in the case of this server, I know that there was a cause and effect. It is the same with our children, if they are acting out in negative behavior, often something is going on in their hearts that they may not be able to express in an appropriate way. Values help us find better ways to process the *cause* so the *effect* can become positive.

Another illustration, as a way of showing you the importance of values, is a story from my community. Several years ago, a windstorm hit my community and several giant trees, which had stood for a hundred years in a park, were blown over. When the park officials investigated to learn why, after all this time, they had fallen, the officials discovered that the trees had been planted too far apart for the type of tree they were. Trees can withstand storms in two ways.

In the first instance, their roots are shallow surface roots but are intertwined, cementing a foundation that helps them stand tall together. They rely on each other to grow and flourish, in the second instance, they have deep taproots that go way down into the bedrock, this allows the trees to bend in the wind without breaking. Often their roots are as deep, as the tree is tall. Both types of root systems are important. The taproot is the stronger solution because it goes deep into the ground and draws nourishment and strength from the water table and rock formations. Weaker trees with shallow roots depend on the large trees with deep taproots to protect them in storms.

Similarly, a family has these two kinds of root systems or values; some are entwined, and some are taproot values that go deep.

ENTWINED/SURFACE ROOTS

In the context of family values, the entwined surface root values are shared values that depend on each other to fulfil. They are negotiated because the individual's values need to be respected while working together to be lived out. The idea is that each person in the family might come from a different position, but they negotiate to gain consensus. For example, if a person in the family has the value of sitting down to eat together at dinnertime. They enjoy the conversation and connection that comes from that special time. However, that value requires agreement by everyone to execute. By agreeing together that the family meal is important, you are entwining your roots. When this value is shared, the family still eats together even when one member is angry with another. I have a strong value of family, and as much as I can I put them first, but what if someone in my family does not share that same value? It can cause problems for me if that value is not shared or entwined with me. As values come from an internal place it is important for each one in the family to share what is important to them and then see where there is overlap. In that overlap you can find agreement. If one has a strong value that others don't, it can be negotiated and in an act of humility and honor the others can follow it to show love to the one who does. In my eating dinner together example, mom may value that dinner time and because the kids are busy with their own things may not, however, to show honour to mom they make every effort to be there. This is how shared values work however there is a deeper level that can be achieved. These are the taproot principals that run deep in your heart.

TAPROOT PRINCIPAL

A taproot principle is internal and is one that cannot be taken away from you and is not dependent on others to live out. These values are the personal convictions that grow in your heart and reflect who you are as a person. Your personhood is shaped by these values, and they protect and guide you during the storms of life. As mentioned above, one example of my personal taproot values is honour. No one can steal that from me. How someone treats me doesn't change my value because I have a deep conviction about being an honorable person. I choose to treat others with honour, no matter how they choose to treat me. In turn, you can see how the taproot of honour supports my vision and mission statements. A family taproot value is the same, it has a deep connection to who you are as a family. Each individual carries the value deep within their own hearts to the point it manifests in the family. An example of that in my family is loyalty, it is a value that is deep in my own heart, but also in my wife and kid's heart as well. This is why even after all we have been through; we are still married. This deep conviction in our heart has spread to our kids. They are fiercely loyal people, not only to our family but to their employers and friends. At the time of writing this our son and his wife have been married twelve years and our daughter and her husband have been married eleven. Our youngest just got married, and we know they will be married for life as well. How can I make such a bold claim? Because they have loyalty as a very high value in their hearts. This is why we could say, as a family, that loyalty was a high family value. Taproots just are, they don't need to be negotiated, they are discovered and known. A family needs to know what each other's taproot values are, so they can honour them but also to discover the overlaps. It is where those values overlap that you will discover what the taproot values are. In the values challenge below it will help you know which are surface roots and which are taproots by the answers each family member has. Remember that surface roots are the values that need agreement with others (external values) and taproots are those values that are deep convictions in your heart (internal values). Below I have provided a list of some of each to help you complete the challenge.

VALUES CHALLENGE

Just as you built vision and mission statements, you should now start thinking about your values. Using the list that follows on the next page as a prompt, work through the steps.

1. Make a copy of the following list for each member of your family.
2. Individually, choose some of the values from the list that stand out to you
3. Decide whether they are taproots (internal values) or entwined roots (external values)
4. Draw a line between matching selections for each
5. Compare your lists to see which values overlap and circles the ones that match up. Choose these shared values for your family because they represent characteristics that are important to all of you.

It's important to note that a secondary strength of this exercise is that you will also see which values are important to others in the family, so you can respect them. However, it's the ones you all agree on which will become the fuel for living out of your family vision and mission.

Now add your values to your poster.

Taproot (internal) Values:	Surface Roots (entwined external) Values:
Affection	Accountability
Generosity	Community
Courage	Family
Gratitude	Friendship
Creativity	Partnership
Forgiveness	Teamwork
Justice	Wealth
Honesty	Sports
Love	Family Dinner
Loyalty	Collaboration
Spirituality	Networking
Wisdom	Communication
Honour	Connection
Integrity	Fairness
Respect	
Kind	… Add your own.

… Add your own.

Ok now that you have finished your framework challenges, you will have a vision and mission statement, you will have an agreed to purpose, and the values to help strengthen the framework that will keep your family moving together into its destiny.

Communicating the framework is essential to developing the culture you desire! There are several tips below to help develop your values into your home's culture. There are many ways to do this, I have shared a few idea's below that I have done with families which got great results.

Creative Displays – As mentioned earlier you can include the kid's in creating art that communicates the family vison, mission and values, hang it up in a prominent spot in the house, even frame it so that everyone that enters can see what your family is all about. You could also create a vison board (a quick google search can help you know how) that communicates where the family is going in the future. Visual reinforcement has proven to be both a great motivator and reminder for people.

Regular family meetings – It is very powerful to set time aside to have family meetings and talk about your values. You want to make it fun and exciting so you could mix games and food with fun activities into the evening. Ask questions around how you have seen each other living the values out. I always encourage parents in my workshops to catch your kids doing right, not always, only catching them doing something wrong. Put a reward system in place to celebrate victories, rewards should also reflect the family values and vision so rewards that align with that is even more powerful. For example, if one of the kids has displayed a living out of the family values well such as being kind, the reward should be the whole family pouring kindness out to them in the form of gifts or affirmation.

Have themed months – You could take each month of the year and align a value with it. During that month the whole family lives out that value in creative ways. Share that value with each other and with neighbors. The month could start with the family meeting highlighting the value of the month. The family can brainstorm together how they could celebrate the value chosen and have rewards at the end for points scored. Points can be gained through activities the family participates in that uphold the value. An example of this in our family is we decided to do a hero holiday one year. We decided, as a family to go to California to serve a homeless shelter we knew there. There would be no tourism or activities that we self-serving only in the service of others. On one of the days, we were handing out sleeping bags to the homeless population. I looked over and saw my six-year-old daughter stroking the head of a homeless woman comforting her as she cried, while receiving her sleeping bag. It touched my heart and made me realize that my kids were getting the family purpose of serving others with compassion. The last day of the trip we rewarded the kids with a trip to Disneyland to celebrate their selfless act of serving others. Sandi and I served them that day by letting them decide on every ride and every activity we did that day as a reward.

Whatever you decide to do make it fun and remember to MODEL, MODEL, MODEL!! These four things: vision, mission, purpose and values will build a fantastic framework for your family to live out. Now the next part of section two is to furnish the home.

CHAPTER 10
FURNISH THE HOME

As mentioned, the framework in a house defines the rooms of the house and how those rooms should be used. Vison, mission, purpose and values do that for your family, However, if you don't furnish those rooms, they are empty and without life. Realtors will tell you how important staging a house is to sell it. The furnishing of the rooms helps you visualize how to enjoy them. There are a few things we need to furnish our relationships and live out all the work you have done so far in this book. Things like knowing each other's love languages, understanding what creates barriers to giving and receiving love, and using strength-based communication all contribute to the beauty of the relationship in your home.

THE LANGUAGES OF LOVE

In his ground-breaking book, Five Love Languages, Gary Chapman lays out that every person communicates in five different love languages. I highly recommend you purchase his book. *www.5lovelanguages.com*

In this chapter, you will discover how to identify your unique love language and that of your family. Often when we express love to each other, it is communicated in our own love language instead of the receiver's. This can lead to misunderstanding and ultimately hurt. I believe that it is extremely important to express the love that we have for someone, but it is equally important to be able to identify when someone is expressing their love for us. Knowing each other's love language helps immensely with this. It is important to note that we all have a few of these, however, the top two are primary to our need to express and receive love.

The descriptions of the five love languages Chapman identifies are as follows:

Physical Touch

A person whose primary language is physical touch is, not surprisingly, very touchy. Hugs, pats on the back, holding hands, and thoughtful touches on the arm, shoulder, or face—they can all be ways to show excitement, concern, care, and love.

Words of Affirmation

Hearing unsolicited compliments mean the world to you. Hearing the words, "I love you," are good, but hearing the reasons behind that love sends your spirits skyward.

Quality Time

Nothing says, "I love you" like full, undivided attention. Really being there—with the TV off, fork and knife down, and all chores and tasks on standby—makes your loved one feel truly special and loved.

Acts of Service

Anything you do to ease the burden of responsibilities weighing on an "Acts of Service" person will speak volumes. The words he or she most wants to hear are, "Let me do that for you."

Giving and Receiving Gifts

The receiver of gifts thrives on the love, thoughtfulness, and effort behind the gift. If you speak this language, the perfect gift or gesture shows that you are known, you are cared for, and you are prized above whatever was sacrificed to bring the gift to you.

You can go online to Gary's Web site *www.5lovelanguages.com* to take the test he has developed to discover what yours are. There is even a kid-friendly version. This is a great exercise for the whole family to do together. It helps you each to communicate in the others' love language, which deepens connection and relationships. As a result, it will strengthen the framework in your family and furnish it with clear communication.

One day, before I understood this, I decided to clean the whole house for my wife. I worked hard for two hours at mopping, dusting, and vacuuming. I wanted to show her that I loved and appreciated her. When she arrived home, she opened the front hall closet and noticed the one dust bunny I'd missed. She announced that house was a mess, and we were going to have to clean it. I felt crushed and could not believe my ears. Later, after reading Gary's book, I discovered her love language was 'quality time' whereas mine was 'acts of service'. I spoke to her in my love language by cleaning when all I had to do was take her out on a date, which would have been much more fun. By the way, a close second for me is words of affirmation, so you can imagine how crushed I was when she said the house was a mess. It seems like a small thing; however, it is so important to understand and communicate in the appropriate love language. In my coaching practice, I have many couples who lament that the other never expresses love to them, however as we talk, and I have them do the love language test, we discover they have all along it just was not received because it was spoken in the wrong language.

LOVE LANGUAGE CHALLENGE

1. After completing the love language test share the results with each person in the family.
2. Write down three ways you could express love in their language in the next week.
3. Have each person in the family practice expressing love in each other's language.
4. Acknowledge when others speak to you in your love language. In other word recognize them for expressing love to you by expressing gratitude to them.

CHAPTER 11
UNDERSTANDING LOVE BARRIERS

In addition to knowing your love languages, it is important to understand the barriers to love that exist in your family. In the hit HGTV show Fixer Upper, the star Chip Gains' favorite part of a house renovation is 'demo day'. He loves tearing out all the old broken things, preparing the space for a fresh, new look. Sometimes in a home renovation (and in a relational makeover), you need to take down some barriers, opening up the relationship to a new design. It's important to know the barriers to expressing and receiving love in your family so you can take them down. Of course, some of the work of removing barriers or walls is about rebuilding the pillars that we talked about in section one. We put walls around our heart to protect it. Those walls, in turn, put barriers up, disabling us from expressing and receiving love. Everyone has a few core needs that are common to all of us. I believe this is because God created us in His image, and so we are a reflection of His nature, and we were designed to reflect that image to each other. Let me explain these common traits in more detail.

God is love – *So we all desire to love and be loved* – Love gives us our significance and our core identity. When love is withheld or missing, we lose our ability to see our own value. When we don't experience love, it makes us feel lonely and vulnerable. We then look to find that significance in other ways that are unhealthy and affect our ability to express or receive love. Often these other ways are destructive and hurt our relationships and our own hearts.

God is Gifted – *We all have gifts and abilities* – Every person has gifts and abilities; I have never met anyone that is not gifted in something. You may be asking how do I know what my gifts are? Well, there are resources out there such as strength finders and gift assessments but the best way to discover what gifts you have is by looking at what you do well naturally. They also enable us to accomplish what we were created to do. A gift is what you're born with, but an ability is the result of practicing that gift until it develops into an ability. I don't know why some people have tons and others, like me, only a few, but everyone has them. It can be genetics or exposer to others with a gift that can develop yours. My son is a gifted drummer, it is certainly not genetic, one day he mentioned to me that he wanted to play and before I knew it, he was playing. He did not have any lessons but watched other drummers, he just picked it up. However, he then got passionate about it and practiced all the time. We never had a problem getting him to practice the hard part was getting him to stop. When you experience pain in life and perhaps are told you are worthless, you lose sight of your gifts and abilities and may even believe you don't have any. I have met many people that believed this lie, and the result was a lack of motivation or confidence. This was the case for me. I felt I was a failure and would never amount to anything. Several things in my life, such as my family dynamic, factored into that belief. School experiences and being told by adults that I was a troublemaker didn't help. I constantly compared myself to others and felt like I was not enough. I ended up putting walls around my heart that affected my ability to believe I had gifts. However, the truth was that I did have gifts, and I have since learned to use them to help others and fulfill my destiny. I also believe that we can use our gifts and abilities to express and receive love. I use mine every day to express love to others.

God is a Creator – *Everyone has hopes and dreams* – I have never met anyone who did not have hopes and dreams. Although, I have met many that have had their hopes and dreams buried by life's circumstances. Once, when I was teaching the Heroes program, with Impact Society, at a juvenile detention center, this belief was truly proven. I told the warden to give us all the worst-behaved kids, so we could prove our program was effective. (I must have been nuts!) The officials obliged. I had six young men in the class that were incarcerated for everything from selling drugs to murder. One young man stood out to me and was clearly the one everyone feared, as he was convicted of murder. His persona was tough, and he used a wall of fear to demand respect. As I shared the content, some that I am sharing with you now, he had his arms crossed and was muttering under his breath. He was clearly agitated. I asked him if he had something that he would like to share. He said, "Yeah, this is BS." I asked him how so, and his answer was, "I don't have any hopes or dreams. I couldn't care less about anything." His response showed that, in fact, he did care. I encouraged him by saying that I believed he actually did have hopes and dreams. They were just buried behind his walls because of his life experiences. A few classes later, he asked to see me privately. We set up an appointment through the counselling office, and I met with him. He told me that I was right, he did have a dream to take over his dad's landscaping business; however, he did not think it would ever happen because of the murder conviction. I asked him to share his story with me and he did. All the other inmates thought he was a hardened killer. His persona helped everyone to think that he was. Although someone's death was his responsibility, it was not the result of a hardened criminal it was actually a tragic accident that was his fault and for which he has huge remorse. He told me that he and some friends had been out drinking, and horsing around, when they came across a gentleman that was walking in the opposite direction. The young man passing, accidentally bumped his shoulder, so he turned around and pushed him. The other guy fell awkwardly, hit his head, and died. In the detention center, this young man had created a persona that he was a scary guy. But really, he was just a teenager who was full of shame and had lost hope. Long story short, I began to work with him to rebuild his dream. As a juvenile, he was able to turn his life around. He now runs his dad's business and employs other kids who have gotten into trouble. It is a story of victory and hope, but it started with reclaiming his dream.

God is Successful – *Everyone has a desire to succeed* – I have never met anyone who sets out to fail. The young man who was doing juvenile time because of a murder conviction did not set out to fail or to hurt someone. He simply made decisions that did not line up with his heart. I struggled with a fear of failure for years, but never did I *want* to fail. Everyone has a built-in desire to do well, however they may not recognize it or could be misinformed on what success is. There are many books written and resources available that can help people to ensure their success, so why do some not use the tools available. In part, our world has gotten confused around what success is. Media tells us that money and fame are what make us successful. Sometimes it is our family of origin putting pressure on us to perform as they think we should. If we get into the right university or have the right career, success can become quite warped. But really, my definition of success is 'doing the best you can with what you have been given'. It is discovering your calling and living it out to the best of your ability. I have a grade eight education and you would see that clearly but for the talented editors who helped with this book. However, I stopped letting fears and excuses stop me from doing my best to live out my calling and destiny.

I heard a story about a man who was a custodian of an elementary school. He worked there his whole career, lived in the neighborhood, and loved what he did. The school had started a reading program at lunch for kids that were struggling with reading. Some parents and other volunteers would go into a classroom during lunch and read with the kids. This man heard about it and volunteered his lunch breaks. He did this for over thirty years until he retired. When he was asked why he stayed at the school so long or why he never sought promotion or to further his career, he answered, "My job was to clean the school, so the students had a clean environment to learn in, and I was good at it, but my career was reading to those kids every week, so they could know the joy of reading a book." **That's success!!** By the way, he read to several generations of kids. He remembered their parents by name and would tell them stories about their moms and dads. The kids would run home and tell their parents what they learned, and there were many chuckles. What do you want to succeed at? Go for it!

You may be asking what all this has to do with relationships. As mentioned previously, when these basic matters of the heart are not met in our lives, we put walls up to protect ourselves. These barriers make it very difficult to actually connect in an emotionally intimate way. Two primary walls pop up when we have not had our core needs met. The two primary walls that can create a barrier to expressing and receiving love are *fear* and *defense*.

FEAR WALL

As mentioned, I grew up in an environment that was very strict and demanded perfect behavior. As a result, I was always fearful that I would fail. I thought I simply didn't measure up in some way. That fear robbed me of believing that I had gifts and abilities or that I could ever succeed at anything, this created a barrier for me to believe I was loved. I don't blame anyone for this. I had just constructed a belief system that I would never be good enough. This belief resulted in my building walls around my heart to make sure no one would ever see that part of me. I made up all kinds of stories about things I'd accomplished but never did, simply so no one would think I was the failure I knew I was. It got so bad that I even started believing the stories and would get very angry when anyone challenged me. This was the reason that I had such a difficult time relating to people. My whole life was a sham, and the walls became barriers that kept me there for many years. The walls affected every relationship I had negatively, which, in turn, convinced me further that I was unlovable and not worth anything. It made me violate the five pillars that are necessary to build that healthy foundation that we've discussed in section one. Fear is a powerful weapon that attacks your soul. Your very essence can be affected by it. Fear stands for **F**alse **E**vidence **A**ppearing

Real. That's why it is so powerful: fear takes partial truths and holds up a magnifying glass to the point of distortion. Fear held a magnifying glass to my failures, declaring them to be the truth about me and attaching failure to my identity. The truth was that because of the wall of fear, I continued to have failures. There were many projects I would start and not finish, many relationships were started but did not last, and fear would tell me it was my fault. When someone would challenge me, the second barrier to expressing and receiving love would come into place. My defensive wall came up, and I would block love from being received.

DEFENSE WALL

When my fear of failure was triggered, my defensive wall would come up. For example, if someone in authority, like a teacher, said I didn't do a good enough job, I would get defensive and fight back. Usually, I lied or became aggressive to stop them from getting too close to my fear. I didn't want anyone to see the real me because I believed it would confirm my fear that I was just a failure. Another example of a defensive wall is pushing people away or never letting them get close to you because you fear rejection. My wife, who had a fear of rejection, pushed everyone away before they had a chance to reject her. Imagine our relationship before we went through healing. Her fear of rejection would activate her defense and she would push me away, which would trigger my fear of failure, and I would get angry to defend myself.

The other way fear of rejection can trigger a defense is to be a people pleaser. You do everything you can to show that you are useful to others. You make decisions that you would never have made naturally just to make people like you. People who struggle with promiscuity are often simply trying not to be rejected. It is a defense that actually does not protect but causes more damage.

These two walls create barriers to giving and receiving love. They become love barriers and keep us from connecting on an emotionally intimate level.

Intimacy = **Into-Me-You-See.** When we put walls around our hearts, we don't allow people to see us. The fact is you still have the desire to love and be loved. You still have those gifts and abilities. There are still hopes and dreams with a desire to succeed, but they are all hidden behind the walls.

Two things happened because of these walls.

First, I was judged by the walls instead of by who I really was. People only saw the walls I put up and so could not understand or see my heart. That's why people label others, there is the bully or there is jerk, and so on. People don't understand the cause and effect of the walls you have. Have you ever been misunderstood? This is why, it is because you are only showing the walls you have put around your heart, and the cycle continues.

Second, I became a prisoner behind those walls. I say this because of the decisions I made in my life. Those decisions that hurt others, but mostly myself, came from the walls, not who I really was. It is crippling and lonely to live behind the walls that are around your heart. I did things I would never have done because of those walls, I hurt people especially those close to me. It led to addiction as I self-medicated under the weight of the façade I had built. I can look back and point to fear and defense as the two primary walls in my life that caused the most destruction, they became my prison. I had to come to a place where I would not allow the walls to stand anymore. You see, only you can decide to take the walls down. You get to choose to live free of the walls. I have sat with hundreds of couples over the years of coaching, whose relationships were falling apart. Almost all of them thought it was the other person who caused their pain. However, when we dug under the surface and looked behind the walls, it was usually discovered to be within their own hearts. The walls they put up were because of a deeply embedded lie they had believed about themselves. Like me, believing I was a failure, the fear drove me to putting barriers up to protect myself.

I can say that most of the time healing starts with self-awareness. These couples came to realize that the way they see themselves is what affects their relationship more then they knew, as well as the fact that their own needs are not being met. The reason no one could ever meet their needs is simply because the walls prevented, even the best-intentioned people in their lives from reaching their hearts. When you take the walls down, you begin to see others in a different light. You are able to begin receiving love without a barrier and your heart begins to come alive once again. Sandi and I came to the place where we could express and receive love from each other on an emotionally intimate level and we have continued to grow together and after 37 years, at the time of writing this, our love is stronger than ever.

You might be asking how do you do take the walls down, where do I start? On the next page there is a Remove the walls challenge that will help you do that.

REMOVE THE WALLS CHALLENGE

Start by challenging your core beliefs about yourself. Dig deep into your heart and answer the following questions. You can enlist the help of a trusted source who knows you well to bounce your answers off of. Ideally this would be your spouse but can be anyone. The idea is to mine for the lies you have believed that caused you to put the wall up.

Ask yourself:
Did I choose this core belief about myself, or did someone else, by their words and actions choose it for me?

Dig into your childhood and think about the negative relational messages that your parents may have unknowingly directed at you through anger or unreasonable discipline. Also, playground bullies sometimes teased you in a way that you believed what they said about you. This is hard work but well worth challenging.

Ask yourself:
Does my current way of thinking about myself, harm me or help me?
Does it help or harm my relationships?

If the answer is yes to either of these, then it is time to challenge and change your belief about yourself.

Ask Yourself:
Is what I believe a partial or the whole truth?

Do this until exercise until you can challenge every core belief that is causing you to create a wall is gone. Until you come to a conviction that you have value. Then you can start rebuilding your core beliefs about yourself.

Once you take the walls down, it is time to start building health into yourself and your relationships. It is time to see the value you have and share your value with others.

Note: if you need help with this process, I offer coaching and you can book through www.markgordon.ca

CHAPTER 12
STRENGTH BASED APPROACH

At the end of the last chapter, you did an exercise on how to remove love barriers. Another way to do this is to begin changing the way you speak to yourself and your loved ones. You want a strength-based approach, which is simply seeing and speaking to people strengths not their weaknesses. Dr. Wayne Hammond has done outstanding work in measuring resiliency in kids. One of the discoveries he made was that people are most resilient when they are spoken to from a strength-based language. To quote Dr Hammond he says, "A strength-based approach develops confidence, character and integrity".

STRENGTH-BASED LANGUAGE

Using strength-based approach is using language that considers the following points.

See what's strong, not what's wrong – often it's easier to see what is wrong in someone rather than what is strong. This is especially true when we are in conflict. If we believe the best of each other, it is easier to see the strengths. Rather than seeing someone as stubborn, we should see him or her as determined. Seeing strengths in yourself and others changes how you speak and treat yourself and others. Rather than saying "you are a so hyper all the time settle down" a strength-based approach would say "you are very energetic and that's great, however it is time to be quiet at this moment".

Label in the Positive – If we must put a label on someone, let's do it in the positive sense. Highlight his or her good points and celebrate his or her personality. Reframe negative labels into positive attributes. You can so this by seeing the value of good things that come from their personality that you would like to have. For example, I was often told as a young person that I was rebellious, however my rebellion was not always rebellion. I was inquisitive and visionary from a young age and would push the boundaries, not because I was rebellious, but because I was always curious about what I could not see. I would ask questions and adults thought I was questioning their authority. I wish they had labeled me as inquisitive; I may not have developed the fear of failure.

Celebrate Individual Personhood – By celebrating individuals, we can celebrate a person's value and uniqueness. We all see things differently, and I find that it is of value to me that my wife sees differently than I do. It's why we make a good team. In fact, unity is not uniformity; it is celebrating diversity. When we celebrate someone's personhood, what makes them unique we give them permission to be themselves.

Affirm Personhood and Contrast Behaviors – We all have bad days and behave badly at times. Those days do not define us, and yet we often identify others by a particular day they acted poorly. What we need to do is separate the behavior from the person, so we can express what hurt us, but not attack the one we love. It is ok to affirm someone and current them at the same time. As mentioned earlier in this book, when my son was a teenager, he went through a phase that he was lying to me about things. When I sat down with him to talk about it, I said "Son you are not a liar so why are you lying to me?" I affirmed that he was a great kid and that he would be loved no matter what and so there was no need to lie.

Avoid Always and Never in Communication – When someone has let us down, we tend to use "always" and "never" language because we are speaking from our hurt. If my son forgets to take the garbage out a few times, it does not mean he always does. When we use this type of disempowering language on people, we are literally putting a curse on them. It is also not true and creates a divide in the relationship. It can cause great harm to a person's self-esteem and does not really get the garbage taken out anyway. It also does not give any room for the other person to improve or give them motivation to change.

Reward Effort, Not Outcome – Everyone has different abilities, but often you expect others to be able to do what you can do or see things you can see. You feel disappointed when someone does not live up to this expectation, which is often unspoken. When you reward effort, it makes that person want to try harder. If you reward only accomplishment or outcomes when they simply don't have the capacity, you cripple their desire to do their best. Having a strength-based approach allows you to see the effort and express gratitude for the effort.

STRENGTH CHALLENGE

In this challenge I want you to reframe some language you have used within the family I have provided a list of a few to help you.

1. Make a list of negative labels you have given each other; Then look at each other and apologize for the relational message that you sent by using those words.
2. Reframe the labels to a positive tense. Look at the strength of the personality trait that goes with it. (the list provided can help)
3. A powerful exercise to do is put each person's name at the top of a recipe card and have each person in the family wright the positive things they see in that person. I have done this with families and with workshop participants and it is a powerful way to communicate value to others.

Negative Labels	Strength-Based Labels
Hyperactive	Energetic
Impulsive	Spontaneous
Stubborn	Persistent
Willful	Independent
Tests Limits	Risk-Taker
Defiant	Bold
Angry	Passionate
Withdrawn	Reflective
Aggressive	Assertive

SECTION 2 SUMMARY

In this section, I have covered many powerful tools to create a healthy relational culture in your home. You have built a strong framework to begin moving forward together. You have created a vision and mission statement, discovered your family purpose and have chosen a set of family values. You learned one another's love languages and removed barriers to experiencing love as a family, finally you are beginning to practice a strength-based approach to doing life together. When you put all these things into practice it will powerfully transform the very heart of the relationships and family. You will experience relationships getting stronger and a very real and tangible change in your family dynamic.

Now that we have done all that great work it's time to put the roof on!!

SECTION 3
BUILDING A STURDY ROOF

The third and final section will provide a protective covering over all the work you have done thus far. It will protect your family in life's biggest storms and keep the home safe when you are struggling through crisis.

In our building a house metaphor, you have discovered how important it is to have a healthy foundation, a strong framework and as you know every house needs a sturdy roof. In building a healthy culture that makes a family strong and fosters healthy relationships, the roof, or as I call it, a covering is very important. Without a proper covering your relationships can get tossed around when the windstorms of disagreement hit, and disappointment starts to brew. A roof does not have much to do with the inner workings of a house it is designed to protect the things in the house. In the same way the strength of a covering for the relationships in your family is generally outside of the inner workings of the family.

CHAPTER 13
CREATING A GREAT FAMILY COVERING

Creating a great family covering is what I call a sturdy roof, and a sturdy roof starts with understanding authority and the role it plays in our lives. Covering simply means 'protection' or 'guiding authority,' for example, a teacher has authority because of their position as teacher and because they have knowledge to pass on that their students don't have. It is important to weave people in authority into the fabric of your family covering. You can do that, by inviting people with authority to speak into the life of the family. This can be done in many ways, you could take a course from an expert, or read a book like this one, that someone with knowledge in an area you need help in. You could join a community group or church, inviting the leaders to provide encouragement and accountability for your family. You can engage a family/relationship coach, or speak with a pastor such as myself, I do both. The wider the network of support and the tighter the connection with those people, the stronger the covering will be. Each person becomes a shingle in the roof. The more accountability you invite into your family relationships, the better they are protected. By inviting feedback, you start to put glasses on your blind spots. You don't know what you don't know. That's why it's healthy to invite others to provide constructive feedback. I did that recently, when I was struggling with some frustration. As a result, I was causing tension in my home, and I didn't realize it. I finally asked a trusted friend and coach to walk me through why I was so frustrated in general. After a few well-placed questions, he announced that I had 'conflict fatigue.' I had never heard that term but now use it all the time. What was happening is that I was involved in several conflict resolution situations with families and organizations at the time. I was involved in so many conflicts for other people that I could not deal with any conflict at home. This resulted in me snapping at my loved ones, which was out of character. Without having someone from outside the family speak into my life, I may not have been able to have seen the problem until greater damage was done. I was not protecting or guiding my family; I was actually hurting them. I have come to understand the power authority carries. Let's look at some different types of authority to better understand it.

Understanding Authority – What or who establishes authority? Authority is established by someone who has the influence, power or position to make decisions for others, or who has knowledge others do not in a particular subject area. Authority is a misunderstood concept and is often used alongside power. Authority is a powerful thing, but it is not to be used as power *over someone*, but rather, to give power *to someone*. Someone who misuses the power their position gives them does not provide authority; they actually undermine it. As mentioned, authority comes through experience and or knowledge someone has in a particular area or a role they possess. Authority is designed to help someone fulfill the responsibility of that role and is meant to protect the people under the authority or covering. When someone has experienced abuse of authority, they may reject all authority, even when its good. This leaves them without protection or a covering. We have all had experiences where someone in a position of power misused the authority that came with it. For example, police officers have a duty to keep the peace. In that role, they are given power, authority and tools to do their job. When the authority is misused, it can actually cause harm, rather than help the people it was meant to protect. If someone has been a victim of misused authority, it becomes very difficult for that person to come under any authority. This circumstance removes the protection or covering that authority was meant to give to an individual or family. The family or organization is now vulnerable to brokenness and hurt. One of the most damaging instances is when a parent misuses their authority. It can be very difficult for that parent's children to come under someone else's authority later in life. As you have read, this was the case in my life and the unfortunate result was I rebelled against any authority and of course the person who was hurt the most was me.

Positional versus Relational Authority – Positional authority is given to someone because of his or her role. As mentioned above, a teacher or police officer has authority because they have been given a job to do. In a family, a father or mother has authority because they are the dad and mom. However, there is a more powerful type of authority, which I call 'relational authority'. Relational authority is earned through developing relational equity. For example, a teacher has authority because of their position, but if they take the time to build a relationship with the students, the students will want to learn and get more out of the lessons being taught. The teacher will also have a greater influence and will bring the best out of the students as a result. When I was teaching the Heroes program in schools, within five minutes of being in a classroom, I could tell if the teacher had relational authority with their students. It was evident by the way the students were behaving and how they interacted with the teacher and visa-versa. Relational authority can be seen in people who care more about the person than the job they are trying to do. In the same way, a family have roles that give a person positional authority, like dad and mom. However, it is the time spent building relationship, and investing in the children's well-being that will determine relational authority. Gone are the days when you have to do something just because mom said to. My kids did what I asked because of our relationship, not only because I demanded it as their dad. I have found, whether at home or work, when I take the time to build relational equity with people I lead, my authority carries far more weight. Authority works best when people with authority walk in humility, know the power or authority they have without having to reach for it. In a very real way, authority brings with it, great responsibility and very needed accountability.

Delegated Authority – Delegated authority is given when someone shares the responsibility of carrying out their role. This means at times you may be asked to do things you need delegated authority to carry out. Within the context of a family covering, authority is given when we, as parents, ask someone else to help with the kids. Coaches, youth leaders, and others may be engaged to help your kids learn new skills. This is delegated authority. For example, I was a youth leader for many years. The parents of those youth asked me to mentor their kids by letting them be a part of our youth organization.

By being placed in my care I had the delegated authority and responsibility to look after these kids. It is no small thing to carry the responsibility of authority in people's lives. It is a great privilege to be given this opportunity and I have always believed in the principal of "who much is given, much is expected." Please note that although I invested in those kids, I could never replace their parents.

When my son was old enough to babysit, he had delegated authority to watch over his sisters. At times, he took advantage of this, abusing his authority. This, of course, resulted in him losing the privilege of delegated authority until he could show us, he could respect it. That is true accountability, many resist accountabilities because they don't want to be controlled or told what to do. However, in a real way, true accountability is simply holding someone to account for what they said they would do or agreed to do.

What is the real purpose of authority? – In its purest form, authority influences and protects. Authority is meant to help someone carry out the responsibilities they have been charged with. It is designed to provide a covering, or in my metaphor, build a sturdy roof over the family or any organization. When everyone understands and respects it, it actually protects the relationships within the family. As mentioned above, weaving people who understand proper authority into your family network is like adding singles to the roof.

AUTHORITY CHALLENGE

1. Is there someone of authority in your life that you have disrespected or not listened too. Make a list of people and send a handwritten note or card to them apologizing and thanking them for their role they played in your life.

   Note: I did this with a former pastor in my life and it was very freeing to me and blessed him

2. Is there someone you have misused your authority with? Write them a handwritten note or card and take responsibility and apologize for your actions. Be specific and authentic.

   Note: I did this with all my kids in my healing journey and have done it with people in my employ. Most misuse of authority comes out of insecurity so this can be hard but well worth the effort.

CHAPTER 14
UNDERSTANDING FAMILY ROLES

Understand roles within the family can help build a sturdy roof because everyone in the family then knows who does what, and it is easier to accept. One of daughters got a promotion to a supervisory role at work but the company did not tell anyone. Because people did not know her role, they did not respect her authority, it undermined her ability to do her job and the negatively affected the overall environment of the office until it is corrected. It is similar in a family, when each person understands their role, they can act intentionally to fulfil that role and the whole family benefits. It also helps raise the respect level in the family which in itself helps protect the family culture. This may seem obvious; however, I would suggest many people do not know their role or at least the responsibility that comes with it. Thinking back to the last chapter if authority comes through the roles we carry, then we must understand the responsibilities that come with the role as well.

Fatherlessness in north America has been identified as one of the greatest contributors to youth addiction, violence and suicide. In my work over 30 years, including with young people, youth experts agree that youth need two things to be emotionally healthy; First is a healthy relationship with both parents, based on trust, mutual respect and non-judgment and the second is having caring adults in their lives who are interacting on issues that are relevant to them. Understanding family roles is vital to a sturdy roof protecting the family.

So, let's have a look at the roles.

Father and Husband – When my son-in-law asked me for permission to court my daughter, my reply was spontaneous. Since then, it has become a foundational teaching of mine. My reply was, "My role as a dad is to protect my daughter's heart and virtue. You are asking me to share in that responsibility. When you have proven that you can do that as well as I can, you will be ready to marry her and then I will pass the baton to you." He, in fact, did prove his ability to protect her, and he married her 11 years ago as I write and they have two amazing children, my grandkids. (brimming with joy in this moment) What I discovered is the role of both a father and husband. We are to be the protectors, providers, and preparers of our families.

As the protector, a father and husband protect the heart of the family by creating a culture that ensures each person has an opportunity to be emotionally healthy. A father and husband provide a stability to the household so all within can feel safe. I have enormous respect for solo parents and as I have coached them, I discovered one of the reasons it is so difficult is that one of the roles that protects the family is missing or put on the shoulders of one person.

I teach a workshop called Nurturing Fathers, and one of the roles a dad has and is misunderstood at times, is that of disciplinarian. Children need discipline, but we have misunderstood the *how to* of discipline. Discipline should be from a restorative place, not a punitive one. Discipline by nature is training; it does not punish. Even the word itself is a derivative of disciple. When we disciple our children, we are making followers of them, so we are shepherds that lead not ranchers pushing the heard. Discipline provides boundaries that teach and protect the kids from harm. If you use it as punishment you are not protecting the children, you are hurting them. Dad's and husbands protect the heart and integrity of the family by making sure the foundation is in place and the framework is being lived out. In short, fathers and husbands are the trusses in the roof that keep the roof sturdy. Of course, your wife shares this characteristic, but fathers have the unique ability to protect.

As the provider, a father and husband provide for the family. The kind of provision I am referring to is not limited to just our financial life but continues to the higher role of facilitating. You are to facilitate the success of everyone in the family, empowering them to succeed at whatever they attempt to do. Parents provide whatever is needed to facilitate that success for their family. My son played hockey, so I provided the inspiration, the equipment, and the training needed to succeed. I would also cheer him on from the stands and would give him tips on how to do his best. The one thing I couldn't do is go play for him. He had to play the game, but I made sure he had everything needed for him to do his best. In the same way, I provide and facilitate everything my family needs to succeed at life.

As the preparer, a father and husband prepare the family for the future. Parents cast a vision for the future and prepare the family to get there. They bring the inspiration and guidance to live out the family vision and mission. They prepare the kids by helping them learn to make good decisions. They prepare them for the storms of life that will come. This preparation is done through intentional time spent with them, lots of effort and a lot of modelling it. Kids catch more than you will ever know by simply watching you.

Mother and Wife – One day when my son was small and still unsure on his bike, he went for a tumble. I ran out to where he fell as quickly as I could to make sure the bike wasn't damaged. I know, I know! But remember, my role is to make sure he has a bike to ride. But as fast as I was moving, his mom knocked me out of the way to scoop him up and comfort him and check him for damage. She took him in, hugging and kissing him, and cleaned up his scraped knee. A mom and wife's role in a family is nurturer, teacher, and guide.

As the nurturer, a mom and wife nurture the family by ensuring everyone's needs are taken care of. They have an amazing capacity to see with a 360-degree view in terms of what the family needs and is doing at any given moment. I am sure you have heard the saying 'mom has eyes in the back of her head.' Moms have an intuition for when things are off or are needing attention. Often, they know what a family member needs before anyone else does including themselves. Moms and wives have a built-in radar or observation abilities that men just don't have. I know that I am generalizing, however I am amazed at woman's ability to be emotionally connected to the needs of the family, they just see things men don't. This comes from a deep well of empathy and a nurturing capacity that puts everyone else first. Mom's and wives put everyone else's needs ahead of her own and should be honoured for it. The result is nurturing culture within the family. This level of care and nurturing builds resiliency in the family that would not be there otherwise. It creates a safe place to live and grow.

As a teacher, mom's and wives pass on knowledge to the family. They love to teach others how to cook, create crafts or learn to make their beds. Moms teach the kids how to navigate life, school, and social interactions. They do this by being good listeners and providing comfort and feedback even when not asked for. Mom's help kids learn to make good decisions by allowing them to experience the consequences of both good and bad ones, and then be ready with a life lesson.

As a guide, Moms and wives guide in being open and accepting of others especially when they are different or hard to love. They guide you through relational landmines, and give survival skills for life, including navigating tricky situations with grace and love. Mom's guide the family through the emotional labyrinth of life. They help kids discover how to stay in touch with emotions while still moving through the pains that happen in life. Moms ask the questions that draw out what is going on inside their children's hearts and then guide them through ideas on how to work through any problems. I was always amazed at how my wife seemed to know everything about the kids before I did. Even today, it seems I'm the last to know. Her discernment or intuition is so sharp that nothing gets by her. These gifts hold the family together and keeps them flowing together.

Child and Sibling – Yes, kids have a role to play in the family, and it is, well, to PLAY! Too often in today's culture we prevent kids from being kids. Media messages and society in general put a demand on kids to grow up too fast. The images and information that kids are exposed to today through media, both television and social has damaged our children in ways we are still discovering. It has robbed kids of their innocence and has created a social awkwardness in kids that makes it difficult for them to interact or connect with peers or adults. The result is, that it is becoming increasingly hard for kids to build healthy relationships. The organization I lead has an after-school care program and over the last decade, I have personally witnessed a breakdown of children's emotional and mental health at an alarming rate. It is far too easy today for professionals to saddle the kids with a label and medication when they are faced with behaviorally challenged children. I believe it actually causes more damage to the child rather than to use a strength-based strategy to help them learn and grow. I often say ADD is truly 'attention deficit' children are starved for attention to the point they have a disorder. A child learns through play; they learn how to interact with others and how to navigate social complexities. Kids learn about boundaries through play, and they discover very quickly when they have crossed one.

Brothers and sisters look out for each other and support each other in hard times. When I was a kid, my brother and I would fight, because I was annoying, according to him. He would get physical with me once in a while when he got mad enough. However, one time I was at school and ended up on the wrong end of a fist. Some older kids were bullying me. Imagine my surprise when my brother stepped in and beat them up, just to protect me! On the way home, I said, thank you, but I also asked, why he stepped in? His answer was, "I'm the only one that gets to beat you up." Many times, I have seen my kids comfort each other when one was suffering from the pains of life or when they were in trouble. They are now all adults with their own families, and they still drop everything and come to the rescue if one of the others is in need. Yes, I am a proud dad! Siblings are comrades and help each other grow and learn. They do this through all kinds of adventures. I remember being terrified to do something but didn't want my big brother to see that I was scared and wanted to do anything he did. I was always trying to be like him and do what he did, I have more than enough scrapes and bruises to prove I couldn't. However, it stretched me, and I learned things I would not have otherwise. I remember one time my daughter was playing on the monkey bars, she had no fear when it came to fun, she wanted to do what the big kids were doing. She fell off the top and broke her elbow to the point she needed surgery to put it back together. They are co-adventurers in discovery and testing the limits of their abilities. My daughter learned a valuable and painful lesson about her limits that day. Kids also teach each other about loyalty and faithfulness, her class rallied around her and called for help then all created a handmade card to cheer her up in the hospital. Her siblings helped her at home as she adjusted to have a huge cast on her arm. Shortly after this we went to a bible camp for a week in the summer. She still had the cast on, and I remember watching the other kids all helping her when she needed it as they went and explored the surrounding woods. They would hold her arm up so she could go into swim because she could not get her cast wet.

As kids play and live together, they are actually learning how to be dads and husbands, moms and wives. When you allow them to work through their struggles with each other they learn how to respect one other in the process. You are teaching them how to create a healthy relational culture in their future homes with their families.

FAMILY ROLES CHALLENGE

I highly recommend a generational blessing to your kids, when it is imparted through a ceremony, it has a powerful result. Recently, I was talking to my son and lamenting about how I wished I could leave him a financial legacy by helping him and his sisters with down payments to buy homes. He responded, "Dad! The legacy you and mom have left us goes way beyond finances. You have left us a family legacy that is rooted in love and honour!" I must admit that I was teary as he was saying this. We all leave a legacy, but what will yours be? You get to choose. Choose well!

In this challenge I suggest having a special family meal and then have a little ceremony after.

Before the meal, Mom and/or Dad in the days leading up to the dinner write out a blessing for each child. To help you, think about the things you love about their personality and character traits you most admire. Think about the things you see that they are really good at and even what you can see for them in the future. When my wife and I did this we even looked up the meaning of their names and were blown away how accurate their names were to who they were. There are books or a simple google search can help you find the meaning of their name. Take all the information and write it out in letter form.

During the meal, talk about the roles in the family. Explain what you have learned in this chapter, in an age-appropriate way, and share the importance of authority and how it protects them. Let them know your role as parents and underline the responsibility that comes with then.

After the meal, Start the Blessing Ceremony, have each child stand in front of the family one at a time and read your letter to them. If you are people who believe in prayer you could then pray for them at the end, have everyone in the family cheer for them before they sit down.

Bonus tip – Mom and Dad could do this for each other, in front of the family. It is a powerful thing when parents bless each other in front of the children. Too often they only hear the fights and arguing. Think what it does for their hearts to hear you bless each other. If a mom or a dad is missing, you could ask a grandparent or someone in your covering to join you. I have done this with solo parent families as a pastor and it is very powerful.

CHAPTER 15
FAITH & FAMILY

I have found through the years that everyone has faith in something, however for me I want to put my faith in something I can believe in, experience and that is more powerful them me. In the context of a covering or in our illustration, a sturdy roof, it makes sense to have someone or something that is more powerful, wiser and who protects us. When I was in recovery, I learned through the 12-step program that acknowledgment of a higher power was key to recovery. I needed a force that was more powerful than addiction to save me. For me, it was believing in Jesus, it was having the revelation that not only did he love me, but he wanted the best for me, and add to that, he had a plan for my life. Faith gave me the courage to begin my healing journey. Faith in God has become a powerful force in our family life ever since. There are three steps of faith that help provide a sturdy roof.

Discovering Faith – Faith is the confidence of what we hope for will actually happen; it gives us assurance about things we cannot see. In my opinion, faith is the currency of hope. This description tells us every family needs faith. As mentioned above, I believe we all have faith in something and a family that harmonizes that faith will grow. My family and I have put our faith in God as we believe He is the one who created us and knows us best. When you have a relationship with the author of relationships, it allows his life to flow into the other relationships in your life. I believe this is why my family has been successful in our relationships. We turn to God in those times we don't know what to do. He gives us the ability to forgive where it may be hard to do so. I've seen over and over again that when people receive His love and guidance, their capacity to have healthy relationships increases. I have also seen many times where it seemed there was no hope, but faith helped people reconcile, restoring relationships and marriages.

You may be asking, "How do I get to know God, or how do I connect with God?" First of all, it's important to know I am not speaking of religion, or a man-made organization. I am referring to Jesus who gave his life for your life. It's as simple as just asking. Ask Him to make Himself known to you, ask him to reveal his heart to you. The Bible, in Romans 10:9 says, "If you confess with your mouth that Jesus is Lord and believe in your heart that God raised him from the dead, you will be saved". Just ask him to reveal himself to you and then to enter your heart and He will. You will feel peace as you never have and will be empowered in your inner spirit. If you want to know more, you can contact me directly through my Web site or find someone you know who has a relationship with Jesus, or call a local bible believing church and set up an appointment with a pastor.

Aligning Faith – Unity is not uniformity; When I was growing up my family of origin did have faith, but it was forced on us and was very religious in nature. It was a set of moral codes that, if broken, punishment followed. It did not allow questions or give space for discovery or interaction. As a result, it was more damaging then good. it is diversity that honors one another's faith. A family does not always agree on every belief, but it needs to honour each other by supporting family members regardless. We don't always have to agree on everything to appreciate someone's point of view. I have always said, "A person with an argument cannot convince someone with an experience." By allowing discussion and discovery, and expressing love and grace, your kids will discover the fruit that faith in God produces, in Galatians 5:22 it says "but the Holy Spirit produces this kind of fruit in our lives, love, joy, peace, patience, kindness, goodness, faithfulness, gentleness, and self-control. There is no law against these things!" WOW think about the family culture with this fruit active in your relationships.

Encourage Faith – by allowing people to have faith, it is important not to squash one another's faith. My kids all live out their faith differently and we have worked hard at allowing them to discover and live out faith on their own. Young children have childlike faith, and you need to allow their faith to grow. When my son was young, he told me that he was going to play in the NHL. I never told him not to believe he would. He did well in hockey, but even if he didn't play in the NHL, I never wanted him to lose faith. He would even include his dream in his bedtime prayer. Although he didn't have a hockey career in the NHL, he has fulfilled many other dreams in his life, because his mom and I encouraged him to believe and ask God for help. By encouraging faith, you are empowering the family, and pointing them to something greater than themselves to help them navigate life's complexities.

For my family, faith has played an integral role in creating a healthy relational culture in our home. It has helped us navigate through some very difficult experiences life has thrown our way. Faith allowed us to come together in crisis rather than drift apart or push each other away. Faith heals you from the inside out, it looks for the best in others, it believes there is always hope for the future. I believe we are all living through a time right now in the world, that needs a fresh injection of faith and hope. You can be the catalyst for faith and hope in your family and in your neighborhood. You can be the change that is needed today!

FAITH CHALLENGE

Find a devotional book in the faith section at your local bookstore, or online versions through kindle and other online bookstores. I like Max Lucado's or Dailey Bread books. There are also great video channels like Right Now Media that have short videos to have discussion starters for your family.

1. After your dinner meal together as a family, read one of the stories, they are usually short about one page long, but provide great insight that builds faith. Get the family to talk about it, what their take away was.

2. Have a family meeting and have mom and dad start by sharing a story of faith, my kids loved our stories of how Sandi and I had to trust God for something saw Him answer our prayer. Then ask the kids to share about their stories of faith with you. Also, bedtime prayers are a very good way to build faith in your kids. Ask them in the family meeting what prayers have been answered.

3. Find a bible believing church in your community and attend a few of their gatherings. It could be a Sunday service or even a home group or special event. You could google search and check them out online first. Families who attend church together grow in faith together. There are many relational based churches out there.

CONCLUDING REMARKS

In conclusion, it is the combination of a sturdy roof, strong framework, and healthy foundation that will make a successful family with a healthy relational culture. When we look at our metaphor of build a house that will stand the test of time, you can now see building a home or family that will stand the test of time and flourish you need to intentionally invest in the three phases presented. It takes hard work and perseverance to do it. I have shared my story throughout this book about how the principals I have shared, and the challenges that went with each chapter, has shaped my family to what it is today. I want to be clear, we, by no means, have arrived and get it perfect. There is no perfect family or a perfect relationship, however the strategies I have shared here have helped us get better each day. When they are applied, we see victory when they are not applied, we see hardship but also get right back to them because they have provided a road map for us.

Each chapter in this book are blueprints towards the healthy relational culture needed to *build a strong family and foster healthy relationships*. Whether it is building a healthy foundation with the five pillars, *trust, communication, authenticity, honesty or honour*. Or building a strong framework by creating a *vision* and *mission statement* and knowing your *purpose* and *values* while communicating in each other's love language with a strength-based approach to the family on a regular basis. Or if it is creating a sturdy roof by inviting others into your family network, adding *shingles* to your roof by having people speak into the life of your family and by discovering and living out faith together, the blueprint will lead you to a great and healthy relational culture in your home.

The same is true for any group of people, whether an organization or a business; these principals will still work. It is the continual, ongoing mastering of these principles that will give you success. In a very real way, this is just the beginning of your journey, not the end of a book.

The more you work through these principles—and the activities, challenges and action steps provided—the more you will see healthy relationships in your life. A healthy relational culture does not just happen. It has to be an intentional effort founded in hope and faith and tons of grace!

FINAL BLESSING

I would like to pray a blessing over you. If you would like to receive a blessing, just read the following prayer, as I have written it, out loud with your family present.

God, thank you for each person who has read this book. I pray that you would bless the relationships within their families. I bless them with the healing of their wounds and mending of what is broken. I bless them with a healthy foundation, a strong framework, and a sturdy roof that will protect them in the storms of life. I bless them with the revelation that you will be the shelter that protects them and that they will discover the love, hope, and faith that is found in you!

Lord, I bless each reader with the knowledge that you love them more than they could ever imagine. I bless each reader to discover your heart for them, so they can enjoy what my family has enjoyed! Amen.

ABOUT THE AUTHOR

Mark Gordon has been a community leader and family coach for more than thirty years. Throughout his career, he has repeatedly proven his dedication to empowering individuals, families, and organizations to become relationally, emotionally and spiritually healthy. Through his current positions of pastor of The Bridge Community of Faith, as a professional speaker, and relationship coach, Mr. Gordon continues to empower people in their daily lives. And as the facilitator of multiple workshops, including Relationship Matters, Strength-Based Parenting, Understanding Anger, Shadow Boxing (Dealing with Shame), he regularly demonstrates his passion for helping people have healthy and happy relationships. For more information on products and services or to book a discovery meeting go to www.markgordon.ca

Mr. Gordon lives in Kelowna, British Columbia, Canada, with his wife of thirty-seven years. He and Sandi have three married adult children and two grandchildren.